- *Isn't it okay to have sex since we're planning to get married soon anyway?*
- *We've known each other for so long. Won't our relationship die if it doesn't develop sexually?*
- *Is God just trying to ruin a good time?*

These are just a few of the common questions Fred Hartley answers honestly in **Dare to Date Differently.** This realistic and practical guide shows us how to be pace-setters in our dating relationships. As we consider these questions, we'll understand our thoughts and emotions more clearly. **Dare to Date Differently** — learn how to *enrich* our relationships.

Dare to Date Differently

FRED HARTLEY

Power Books

FLEMING H. REVELL COMPANY
OLD TAPPAN, NEW JERSEY

Unless otherwise identified Scripture quotations are taken from the HOLY BIBLE: NEW INTERNATIONAL VERSION. Copyright © 1973, 1978 by the International Bible Society. Used by permission of Zondervan Bible Publishers.

Scripture quotations identified KJV are from the King James Version of the Bible.

The Scripture quotations contained herein identified RSV are from the Revised Standard Version of the Bible, Copyrighted © 1946, 1952, 1971 by the Division of Christian Education of the National Council of the Churches of Christ in the United States of America, and are used by permission. All rights reserved.

Scripture quotations identified PHILLIPS are from THE NEW TES-TAMENT IN MODERN ENGLISH, Revised Edition—J. B. Phillips, translator. © J. B. Phillips 1958, 1960, 1972. Used by permission of Macmillan Publishing Co., Inc.

"Love Is Not a Feeling," by Don Francisco, copyright © 1982 New Pax Music Press/ASCAP. All rights reserved. Used by permission of the Benson Company, Inc., Nashville, TN.

Library of Congress Cataloging-in-Publication Data

Hartley, Fred
    Dare to date differently / Fred Hartley
    p. cm.
    Summary: Advice for daring to date within Christian boundaries. Includes discussion questions.
    ISBN 0-8007-5266-X
    1. Dating (Social   customs)—Religious   aspects—Christianity. 2. Sexual ethics. 3. Youth—Sexual behavior. [1. Dating (Social customs) 2. Sexual ethics. 3. Christian life.] I. Title.
HQ801.H337 1988
306.7'34—dc19   87-29498
                                                                CIP
                                                                AC

Copyright © 1988 by Fred Hartley
Published by the Fleming H. Revell Company
Old Tappan, New Jersey 07675
Printed in the United States of America

TO some very special members
of my family:
John and Lee Carter
Debbi-Jo, Rebecca, and Robby Dykstra
Brad, Kristy, and Betsy Huizingh
Jenifer, Joel, and Jodi Larson

Contents

Dare to Date Differently

one

Hayrides and Miniskirts

Everywhere across our country from the state university to the small-town junior high, students are waking up to the fact that we need to start dating differently. The question is: Who will make the first move? Likewise, what are the alternatives? We might not like the oldy-moldy, outdated methods of courtship, but who has any new ideas?

Believe it or not, we will discover that there are many exciting ways to date differently and avoid many heartaches in the process. And we will meet many pacesetters who are leading the way.

The Hayride

When I was in the ninth grade, a church hayride was announced, and I got all excited. I wondered, *What do Christian girls do on a hayride?* I looked around, spotted the cutest girl in the church, got up enough courage, and asked her to go with me. Her name was Dawn and she accepted.

Anthony Campolo, sociologist and comedian, made a profound observation about Christian hayrides: "There's usually one guy with a guitar singing 'Do Lord, O Do Lord' while the other kids are doing it." Well, Dawn and I were singing three-part harmony with the guitar player.

The hayride was about twenty minutes old, and Dawn and I were having a lot of laughs. Things were going so well I figured it was time to try something harmless like holding her hand, so I put my hand on top of hers. Without even looking at me, she slid it away like a roach crawling out from under a log. Strike one.

Later I convinced myself it was worth trying again, so I positioned myself a little closer and put my arm around her shoulder. This time she stuffed hay between us and giggled. I was convinced she was either a nerd or some creature from outer space. Strike two.

My final move came at the end of the evening. I can still

remember it vividly. My dad drove us to her home; I walked her to the front door. The moon was full, the neighborhood was quiet, her parents were nowhere to be found, and my dad's car was parked around the side of the house out of view. Everything was perfect! *She was just playing hard to get,* I told myself. *Now's the time . . . it couldn't be better.*

As we got to the door, she looked up at me with her large eyes glistening in the moonlight and smiled. I was sure she was saying to herself, *Whatcha gonna do now, hot shot?* I boosted my confidence by telling myself, *Go for it! What do you have to lose? What could possibly be wrong with a little kiss? She'll love it*

I gave her my Joe Cool smile, as if to say, *You'd better hang on, sweetheart, I'm gonna knock your socks off,* tilted my head slightly, took aim at the center of her lips, and moved in for the kill. Before my lips hit the target, she reached out without batting an eye, grabbed my hand, shook it firmly, and said, "Fred, I had so much fun with you tonight, I wouldn't want to ruin it. Thanks for everything. I hope we can do it again sometime. Good night." Strike three.

She turned, went inside, and when the door was shut, I was left standing there in the moonlight, feeling like a misfit. I walked back to the car with my head hanging down like a rookie who had just struck out on three pitches. I would have felt better if she had hauled off and slugged me. At least then I would have had the satisfaction of knowing that she was the nerd, not me.

When I got in the car my dad, famous for his one-liners, said, "Boy, that was fast!" I just grunted. I was stunned. I didn't know what hit me. I didn't even know what I was up against. I felt like building one of those contraptions where you pull the lever and it kicks you with a boot in the rear end.

Through that painfully embarrassing experience, I began to realize for the first time in my life what values are. That night I was not just dealing with a religious fanatic or some creature from another planet. It was far more complex than that. I was butting heads with someone who so valued her moral convictions over her popularity that she was willing to risk friends and even her reputation. You could say she was the first girl I knew who dared to date differently. Even though I thought Dawn's convictions were a boring drag, I was impressed with how firmly she held to them and how normal she was in spite of them. At the time I certainly hated to admit it, but there was obviously a strength in her life that was not only admirable but very attractive.

Dawn was a pacesetter. She was popular at school, and yet she obviously was not caught up in playing all the dumb little social games.

Yes, I asked her out again. Yes, she accepted. Yes, I tried for another kiss. No, it was not successful. What can I say? I guess I'm a slow learner. Nonetheless, I must admit, that hayride taught me more about values than all the sermons I had heard.

I tell this story not to suggest that holding hands or putting our arms around each other or even kissing is wrong. There are certainly bigger issues to deal with than these. But I share this story because Dawn was a very positive example to me. She taught me that we all need to draw the line somewhere between what we will do and what we will not do while dating. Otherwise, we are just a bunch of wimps.

The Light Side

Dating is a blast! It is a fun and important part of growing up.

It is hard to tell when it happens, but usually sometime in junior high school we develop a strange new attraction to the opposite sex. For the first time boys decide that girls are more interesting than frogs. When that happens, it is a sure indication the change has started. Once the invisible switch is flicked, there is no turning back. Frogs will never again be as attractive as girls.

This attraction shows itself in many obvious ways. We do things with each other that would have bored us to tears when we were younger.

- We talk for hours on the telephone without really talking about anything.

- We write notes to each other.
- We doodle graffiti on notebook paper or desk tops, such as, "I love Sherry" or "F.H. + S.D. forever" inside drawings of hearts and arrows.
- Guys tell jokes that look for a greater response from the girls.
- We dress cool to make a good impression.
- Girls shower longer, brush longer, curl longer, and groom longer.
- We buy the right cologne, toothpaste, and skin lotion.
- We shave for the first time.
- We exchange smiles, rings, bracelets, and school pictures.

Discovering the opposite sex can be as exhilarating as discovering America. It is no less exciting than climbing Mount Everest and no less significant than inventing the light bulb or harnessing nuclear energy. Sparks fly. Palms sweat. Hearts thump faster. It is all part of the wild, wonderful world of learning to date.

The Heavy Side

Dating is also horrifying! It can be the most insecure part of our growing up.

I will never forget the first night I met Wes. He was a 220-pound hunk. He drove up in a gigantic white Jeep with huge chrome mag wheels. It was jacked up so high you could walk underneath it without bending over. He looked like the kind of hard guy who would pour milk and sugar on a bowl full of nails and eat them for breakfast. He wore an undersized tank top, and his muscles popped out all over the place. He had more hair under his arms than I had on my head. He had three of the cutest girls hanging all over him. He looked like a tag-team wrestler. He already had his cheering section. But I would certainly never get in the ring with him!

We played soccer that night with about twenty other friends. I made sure I was on Wes's team. We won easily.

Later that night when we were leaving I couldn't believe my

eyes. Wes came up to me with tears running down his face. He was blubbering like a baby. He asked if we could talk. I was not about to say no. My curiosity was killing me. *What could reduce a monster like this to tears?* I wondered.

We slipped away, and he spilled his guts. "Sally won't even talk to me," he choked out the words. "Man, it's killing me. I try to be so nice to her, and she doesn't even know I'm alive. I think she likes George."

We talked for a little while. He said it did him some good, and he thanked me. As I drove home that night, I shook my head in amazement at the heartaches caused by the dynamics of dating. I thought, *If Wes gets so wiped out over girls, what chance does the average guy have? And worse yet, what about the nerds?*

Girls face just as many insecurities.

- Growing hair on new parts of their bodies.
- Popping pimples.
- Hearing rumors and gossip about themselves.
- Feeling threatened and inferior and outclassed.
- Having fat thighs and small breasts.

Discovering the opposite sex can be as overwhelming as flunking chemistry. It can be as depressing as a flat tire and as embarrassing as spilling catsup on our laps. There is no question about it, dating has caused more teenage tears to flow than all other hurts put together. One high school couple in New York broke up because of a misunderstanding. They were both so upset about it, within seven days they individually committed suicide.

Dating is one of the most blessed and the most cursed areas of our lives.

The Miniskirt

By the time I was a senior in high school, I had learned a few things about dating, and I had established certain standards for myself. I decided what I would and would not do on a date.

I would not put myself in the pacesetter category, but I was at least a few levels above wimp.

Somehow I got a date with Sandra. She was a knockout. As far as I was concerned, she was the prettiest girl I'd ever seen. As I drove to pick her up, I was quoting some radical words of Jesus in my mind, *"You have heard that it was said, 'You shall not commit adultery.' But I say to you that every one who looks at a woman lustfully has already committed adultery with her in his heart. If your right eye causes you to sin, pluck it out and throw it away; it is better that you lose one of your members than that your whole body be thrown into hell. And if your right hand causes you to sin, cut it off and throw it away; it is better that you lose one of your members than that your whole body go into hell"* (Matthew 5:27–30 RSV).

Suddenly I realized Jesus was talking about a very strict moral standard. *I know how much I value my hands and my eyesight,* I thought. *There is no way I would ever cut off my right hand or gouge out my right eye from its socket.* [Jesus was not recommending that anyway.] *Jesus made it clear that sex outside of marriage is not only wrong but even thinking about it is wrong. In fact, just looking at an improperly dressed woman should be so horrifying to us that we should prefer plucking out an eye or amputating a hand. Wow! That's strong stuff!*

I pulled into her driveway, got out of the car, ran up the sidewalk to her front door, and rang the bell. Sandra jumped through the doorway with a giant smile and said, "What do you think?" as she spun around to show off her new outfit. My eyes bulged out. My jaw fell open. My cheeks turned red. Her skirt was shorter than a mini—I'm talking micro!

Inside my head I panicked, *Oh, no! I can't believe this is happening to me. What do I say?*

By the dumbfounded expression on my face, she could tell we were on drastically different wavelengths. At moments like this I am not known for my subtlety. I blurted out, "It is either my plucking out my eye or your changing your dress." I couldn't believe I actually said such a thing to such a popular girl. I was in too deep already so I continued, "If you don't mind, I would really like you to change your dress . . . I'll stay down here and wait for you in the car."

Even though the poor girl was certainly embarrassed, she got the message—like getting hit with a freight train. As I waited for her to change, I thought back to my hayride experience. I remembered feeling like a total slob, but I thought about how much I learned that night. Besides learning how to eat humble pie, I learned about values and about how a Christian doesn't just go along with the popular trends. When Sandra was still upstairs in her bedroom changing, I thought, *Wow! If there is any way I can help reprogram her value system, I am willing. As Dawn helped me, maybe I can help Sandra.*

Two months passed since that memorable evening with Sandra. I was hesitant to ask her out again. The phone rang. It was Sandra. "Fred, I just wanted to thank you for taking a stand. I am a new Christian. All the guys I've ever dated expected me to dress like that. But you were different. I must admit, at first you scared me. I was even mad at you but I'm over it now. I realize that I need to start living differently and dating differently. Jesus is in my life now, and I want Him to be pleased with me."

When we hung up, I sure felt good. It felt good to know that Sandra was learning that as a Christian she needed to date differently. And I must admit, it was also nice just to get a phone call from her.

My Wife, Sherry

When I was in high school, I hated to read. In fact, I graduated from high school without having read one book of assigned reading (a distinction for which I am not exactly proud). Rather than studying, I did a lot of dating.

By the time I got to college, I needed to buckle down and study, so I was a card-carrying bachelor. Everything was cool. I was committed to going to sleep early, getting up early, and studying hard—that is until I met a girl named Sherry Dykstra. Somehow every organ in my body told me I had met my match. It seemed that my plans for professional bachelorhood were suddenly a big joke.

Soon after we started dating, I went to the local Christian

bookstore and bought every book they had on dating—sixteen books! I learned to read in a hurry, but the books were disappointing. I could put all of them into two piles. One group was outdated. They were written by eighty-five-year-old college professors trying to tell me about "the teenagers of today." The content was okay, but their words were so long I needed a dictionary in order to understand their meaning.

The other group of books were written by younger authors who spoke my language, but they told me it was okay to do things on dates I already knew were wrong. Unfortunately, neither stack of books did me much good.

The pleasant discovery I made, however, was that the Bible had much to say about dating. Sometimes we might think, *What does Jesus know about this subject? After all, He never dated.* True, He never dated, but He created us and He made us so that we would enjoy relationships with the opposite sex. No one has a higher view of sex and morals than God. He knows what we need, and He knows what we need to flee like the plague. He has set down standards in order to protect us from the bumps and bruises so we can enjoy a full and exciting life.

Sherry Dykstra and I are now married. We have been married for fourteen years, and we are still as excited about each other as we were in college. I am certainly glad we took our dating relationship seriously. It was not perfect, but we avoided many common problems.

Perhaps it seems light-years away, but someday you might also choose marriage. As important as that marriage choice will be, it is also important to make right dating choices now. Dating is where too many people are making major mistakes. Some of those mistakes are ruining lives.

The patterns of dating we see practiced around us are shabby. Some are outdated, and others are completely off the wall. In the next chapter we will discover just how shallow popular dating trends really are.

For Discussion

1. Did you ever have an experience like the one the author
   had on the hayride?
   Have you ever dated a girl (or guy) with strict standards?
   How did that person make you feel?

2. Have you ever "fallen in love"?
   Describe the feeling.
   What effect did it have on you?

3. Did you ever get hurt from breaking up?
   How did it happen?
   Why did it hurt so badly?

4. Do you get nervous before a date?
   Even if you only get a little nervous, explain the feeling.
   Why does it sometimes happen?
   Why does it sometimes *not* happen?

5. Have you ever had an experience like the author did
   with the girl in the micromini skirt?
   Have you ever stood up for moral principles, while
   dating?
   Describe the situation.
   Are you glad you did?
   How did it make you feel about yourself?

6. Have you ever given in to pressure, when you knew it
   was wrong?
   Describe the situation.
   How did *that* make you feel about yourself?

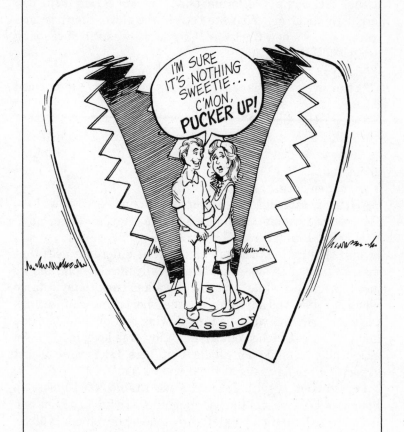

two

Caught in the
Dating Squeeze

B *brrnngg!* The phone rang. It was my girlfriend Joan. I was hoping she would call. It had been two weeks since she had left for vacation in California, and I was wondering if she had forgotten about me. We were both in the eleventh grade, and since she was a new Christian, I hoped she was still developing her friendship with Jesus.

"Are you having a good time?" I asked.

"Yeah, everything is okay," she answered. Her voice sounded flat.

"What's the matter?"

"Well, there is something bothering me. . . . Tonight I was sitting on the beach, watching the sun go down . . . thinking about you. . . ."

"So far so good," I chuckled.

"This guy came up to me. Everyone around here knows him. He stretched out his arms to me and said, 'Hey, free love, lady?' I told him I didn't even know him . . . that we'd never met before. He just laughed and said, 'What difference does that make? C'mon, free love, lady?' He is really nice looking, and we just talked for a while, and then I walked back to my cottage alone. We didn't do anything, but the whole thing confused me. I can still see him with his face glowing and his hair blowing and his arms stretched out saying, 'Hey, free love, lady?' I feel sick inside. I feel like I'm all alone out here. Like everyone just expects you to have sex at the drop of a hat."

I could identify with Joan. She and I talked for at least an hour, and I did most of the listening. She was full of doubts and fears and insecurities. She felt threatened. She felt out of place, like an oddball or a freak. I wished I had answers for her, but at the time, I did not.

Can you identify with Joan? Have you ever felt confused about sex and love and where to draw the line? Have you ever felt as though you were the only one among your friends with a moral standard? Have you ever felt pressured to compromise?

Endangered Species

Face it, virgins are in the minority. In fact, they are on the list of endangered species.

People magazine (April 13, 1987) did an extensive survey of 2,900 high school and college students and 500 parents of teenagers across the country. They put together some figures that were alarming

- 57 percent of high-school students are not virgins
- 79 percent of college students are not virgins
  Teenagers first have sexual intercourse at the average age of 16.9
- 33 percent of high-school students have sex at least once a month
- 52 percent of college students have sex at least once a month
- 53 percent of teenagers consider abortion to be the best solution for an unwanted pregnancy
- 81 percent of the parents thought they were getting honest answers when they talked with their teens about sex
- 25 percent of the teens said they give their parents honest answers while talking about sex

These statistics indicate that if I am a virgin, I am in the minority. If I hold to a moral standard that says I will not have intercourse until I am married, I will probably be treated like a weirdo, and I will certainly feel pressure to compromise. Further, this survey showed that parents are out of touch with their teens. Young people are not telling the whole story to their folks.

Our Sex-Saturated Society

Our generation is suffering because the very special area of human sexuality has become commonplace. What should be confined to the bedroom is now chanted in the streets. What was designed only for marriage is exploited everywhere else We are bombarded with sex talk, sex jokes, sex pictures sex songs, sex magazines, sex movies, sex cartoons, sex billboards, and dial-a-porn.

Porno pictures are as easy to collect as baseball trading cards. We can get front views, side views, back views, top views, and bottom views. Today we can watch in our living rooms what would have been an embarrassment to watch in the movie theaters only a few years ago.

Pornography has not only infiltrated advertising, magazines, literature, but also music. What started as suggestive is now explicit. Van Halen sings their song "Hot for Teacher." Prince gyrates on stage in front of drooling fans and bounces from one sexual pose to another. Judas Priest sings "Eat Me Alive," presumably about oral sex. Motley Crue sings "Live Wire," about sex and violence.

Even perfume companies are resorting to twisted brand names. Calvin Klein has a new scent called "Obsession" and Christian Dior has one called "Poison."

So many of our sports stars, Hollywood heroes, and favorite rock musicians have had illegitimate children. It is no wonder Rod Stewart admitted, "I thought everybody in rock 'n' roll had illegitimate children." Goldie Hawn, who has had three illegitimate children with her live-in lover, says, "Marriage is ridiculous."

Gene Simmons of the rock group KISS says, "Our music is concerned with sex and little else." Jacques Morali, producer for Village People, says, "I am sincerely trying to produce songs to make gay people more acceptable" (*Human Events*, February 23, 1980).

Mick Jagger, lead singer for the Rolling Stones, said, "Rock 'n' roll is not a tender medium; it's rowdy and macho. There is no such thing as a serene family-oriented rock 'n' roll song. In actual fact, I love women; I'm absorbed by them, and if you ask any of my women friends, not just the ones I've had affairs with, they'll tell you that I'm very nice."

Many of us have chosen perverted heroes. Just because someone gets his face on a magazine cover doesn't mean his life is worth modeling. Just because she stars in movies or sells a million records doesn't make her an authority on anything. Before we start playing follow the leader, we need to be careful about who is at the front of the line. If their lives are morally messed up, it might be time to get out of line. It might be time to find a new hero.

The Vice Vise

A *vise* is a carpenter's tool with two jaws that open and close with a screw or lever used to squeeze materials firmly and hold them in place.

A *vice* is an area of moral failure—a bad habit.

Dating has all too often degenerated into a vice vise. It frequently squeezes us into immoral behavior, and when that happens it squeezes the life out of us.

A seventeen-year-old girl in Illinois told me, "I just wanted to get it over with. I was sick and tired of getting teased for being a virgin. I just wanted to say I had done it. Now I hate myself for it. But it's too late." She was caught in the vice vise, and she couldn't handle the pressure. She made a decision to give in to her boyfriend, and he took her for all she was worth.

We have all heard friends say things like:

- "If it feels good, do it."
- "Anything goes—don't deny yourself any pleasures."
- "You can do whatever you want as long as no one gets hurt."
- "Sex is great; so the more the merrier."
- "Moral taboos are taboo; they only get in the way."
- "If you marry someone before you have sex with him, how do you know you're compatible?"
- "Virginity is a sickness; help stamp it out."
- "If sex with the opposite sex is good, why not sex with the same sex?"
- "Everybody else is doing it, why not you?"

This vise of immorality tries to put the squeeze on all of us. Like a successfully hidden bear trap, many naive, innocent friends have smelled the bait, walked too close, and have been caught in the process. Many are fighting desperately to get out, but they don't know how.

The Jaws of Compromise

I met a scuba diver who told me the incredible story of what happened while he was diving under a bridge in the Florida Keys. He saw the enormous head of a jewfish sticking out from under a ledge. He estimated the fish to weigh at least five hundred pounds. He got so excited that he swam to the surface to notify his diving buddy and to get their power-head—a spear-gun-like rod with a twelve-gauge shotgun shell in its end. As he swam back to the spot where he had seen the huge fish, he was unable to spot it the second time. He swam under the ledge to take a look and . . . CRUNCH! The next thing he knew, he was being crushed, twisted, and bent in half.

When his buddy swam down to join him, all he could see were two hands and feet sticking out of the mouth of a gigantic jewfish. The power-head was lying on the bottom. Instantly, he knew what happened. When the jewfish opened his enormous mouth, it created such a vacuum that everything near the opening got sucked inside—even the scuba diver!

The second diver retrieved the power-head, popped it into the skull of the fish, which in turn spit out the first diver who had been bent double for at least five minutes. Both men then swam very slowly to the surface, drove their boat back home, and have not been diving since then. The man showed me the scars on his forearms and calves which continually remind him of the dangers of becoming overinvolved in a sport while underestimating its risks.

I think about all the teenagers who have underestimated the moral risks of dating and became overinvolved with their partners. Before they realized what happened, they were sucked into the jaws of compromise. They did what they never intended to do until they were married. They were mutilated by casual morals, and they have the scars to prove it.

The sucking action of our generation is powerful. At times it resembles the fat head of an old jewfish. It seeks to strip us of convictions and get us to compromise our principles. We need to be alert to the dangers of dating before we become overinvolved in a relationship.

Spring Break

A student at Clemson University came home for spring break this year. She told me that posters plastered all over campus alerted students to the hard facts: "One out of five college students who goes to Fort Lauderdale over spring break will sooner or later die from AIDS."

She said, "My friends and I were planning on going but after all the warnings, none of us went." Then she added, "Last year virgins were laughed at. This year they are admired. Everyone wants to date a virgin. No one wants to marry someone carrying AIDS. We used to look at dating as a big game, but now everyone is much more serious about it."

College and university students are waking up to the fact that the popular patterns for dating have not worked. They are now beginning to recognize that free sex is a lie. Sex is never free. There is always a price to sex, and there is always a commitment involved. The price is a lot higher than most of us realized.

I laughed out loud reading an article on the editorial page of the *Miami Herald.* "Since AIDS can now be transmitted heterosexually as well as homosexually, the only way to be sure you won't get it is to remain a virgin, marry a virgin and remain faithfully married to that same person." Brilliant deduction! That is precisely what God has been saying for four thousand years. Perhaps our generation is waking up to the fact that the fling of a one-night stand needs to stop. Perhaps our generation is prepared to rediscover the exciting style of dating God sets forth in the Bible.

AIDS is only one of the diseases spread sexually. There are actually millions of Americans who have at least one of the twenty-five sexually transmitted diseases.

According to *Liberty Report,* in 1985 alone, there were 27,143 newly reported cases of syphilis, 910,895 cases of gonorrhea, 1 million cases of urethritis, 1.2 million cases of mucopurulent cervicitis, and 4 million cases of chlamydia.

That is not all. It is estimated that between 5 to 10 million people have genital herpes and 25 to 40 million have genital warts. If cures are found to eliminate the symptoms of these sexual diseases, worse strains will break out. Already it has been discovered that a cancer virus is being communicated through sexual immorality.

What is even worse than this huge list of physical problems caused by sexual misconduct are the countless broken hearts and broken marriages in the wake of the sexual revolution. Self-esteem has been left strewn all over the landscape. Guys have been left stripped of moral strength and character and girls likewise have been left feeling empty, barren, and unful-filled.

The Bible says, "Flee from sexual immorality. All other sins a man commits are outside his body, but he who sins sexually sins against his own body" (First Corinthians 6:18). Sexual sins leave those involved feeling raped and cheated even though 99.9 percent were voluntary victims.

Help!

Most of us have felt at some time like my high-school girlfriend Joan as she sat on the beach in California—out of place and all alone. The pressure to compromise has grabbed us and squeezed us. We have felt confused, frustrated, and trapped. At times we wanted to jump up and scream *Help!*

Virginity might become popular one year and then unpopu-lar the next year. Popularity comes and goes. We need to understand that *wrong is wrong even if everyone is doing it, and right is right even if no one is doing it.*

The reason dating patterns are so shabby is because the standards of right and wrong have been thrown out. When all standards of moral excellence are removed, we settle for sloppy dating and substandard living. In the next chapter, you will see what I mean.

For Discussion

1. Like Joan, on the beach in California, have you ever
   felt pressured to lower your standards?
   Have you ever felt as if you were the only one to have
   moral standards?
   Describe the situation.

2. How are virgins treated in school?
   Is it popular or unpopular to be a virgin?

3. What percentage of your friends have not had intercourse? Just guess.

4. Have you ever heard music with "sex lyrics"?
   Which songs, by which groups?

5. What kind of music do you like?
   Which is your favorite group?

6. Which was your favorite movie?
   Why did you like it?
   Have you ever walked out of a movie because it was
   immoral?
   Did you ever feel like it?
   Which movie?

7. Are there standards we could use to determine what
   music is worth listening to?
   Are there standards we could use to determine which
   movies are worth attending?

8. Does the fear of getting AIDS motivate anyone to
   abstain from sex?
   Does it affect you?

9. List the three most common reasons why your friends
    have sex outside of marriage.

10. List three reasons why it is a good idea *not* to have sex
    outside of marriage.

three

Life Without a Moral Standard

A young person without a moral standard is like a cow going to slaughter. Each of us must have a standard of sexual conduct, determining right and wrong, or else before long we might find ourselves chopped up like hamburger meat.

The word *standard* has several interesting dictionary definitions: (1) an established unit used as a basis of comparison to measure value or excellence; (2) any upright object used as a support or stand; (3) an agreed-upon pattern used as a model or example.

Standards are yardsticks, thermometers, scales and other instruments which help us measure the quality and value of different products. Moral standards are instruments which help us determine the quality and value of life.

Standards are used in construction to support weight and strengthen walls. They are capable of withstanding great pressure and protecting against collapse. Likewise, moral standards protect us from the pressure of the crowd that wants us to compromise our convictions.

Standards are generally understood guidelines that help us select our hairstyle, clothes, and music. They help us choose between a good car and a piece of junk. Moral standards are guidelines that help us select our friendships, boyfriends/girlfriends, and our life-style. They help us choose between good and raunchy conduct.

We can easily see that society would not function for long without standards. It should be equally apparent that our personal lives will not survive for long without moral standards.

In a day when 57 percent of high-school students and 79 percent of college students have had sexual intercourse, when at least one out of ten fifteen-to-nineteen-year-old girls gets pregnant, and when there are at least 10 million cases of active venereal disease, it takes little imagination to recognize that something needs to change.

In the late sixties and early seventies, every traditional

moral standard was challenged. Morals were seen as excess baggage and useless to society. When people wondered where these moral standards came from, no one seemed to remember, so they were crumpled up and thrown in the dumpster. Our generation is the first generation in a few hundred years without a moral standard, and we have therefore suffered badly.

Three Friends

Three of my friends told me their stories this way.

Tim, freshman at University of Southern California
"I've messed up bad. I first had sex in eighth grade. I thought it was cool. We'd go to the beach and party. I got into drinking and smoking pot. My older brother and sister were doing it. I was sort of a hero with my friends. I know I've hurt a lot of people along the way, including myself, and I want to stop. I want somebody to show me some guidelines. Can you help?"

Gina, eleventh grade in Burlington, Vermont
"I've been dating this guy for two years. It's like he's got me wrapped around his little finger. Both our parents are Christians and we are active in the youth group and everything. That's why I feel like such a hypocrite. Nobody knows—at least I hope nobody knows—but we've been doing it for the past year. Last month I thought I was pregnant. I almost died! I know we can't keep going like this, but I don't know how to stop."

Cindy, twelfth grade in Memphis, Tennessee
"I can't stand it. I got pregnant with a guy I hardly knew. I always thought it would happen to someone else—not me! I thought my parents were going to kill me. They made me get an abortion. Inside I feel so empty. That was a year and a half ago, and I haven't dated since. I'm scared and I don't trust anyone—not even myself. I can't afford to go through that pain again. Do you think things will ever change?"

*   *   *

All three of these friends got in over their heads before they realized what was happening. They all felt old and burned out, and none of them had even celebrated his or her twentieth birthday. Friends told them sex was great, but that was only half the story. All they heard about was the thirty-minute sizzle. What they didn't hear about was all the pain and scars and fear and guilt to follow.

These three friends represent a majority of our generation who have also believed the lie and have become overinvolved in relationships before they established a moral standard. They have had to live with the consequences.

Sour-Milk Relationships

One day I came inside after working in the yard. It was 92 degrees and I was sweating like a hog. I poured myself a tall glass of cold milk, put a few chocolate-chip cookies on a plate, and sat down at the kitchen table to enjoy my refreshment. I was so thirsty I lifted the glass to my lips and started guzzling. Not until I drank half the glass did I suddenly realize the milk was sour. *Sick!*

I ran to the sink and spit out every drop still left in my mouth. But most of it was already in my belly. There was no way to get it out. Even though I was willing to vomit, I couldn't. It was too late. I felt sick.

Had I not been in such a hurry, I could have noticed the strange color of the milk and the small curds or even the bad smell, but I failed to use the common standard of judging milk. My lustful thirst took over, and I suffered for it.

It is possible to indulge in sour relationships before we know what is happening. We commit ourselves, become intimately involved, and before we realize what is happening, we feel sick inside. The relationship is okay. The commitment and desire for intimacy is okay. But without paying any attention to a moral standard, we will suffer for it.

Horror Stories

The scars left on young hearts take longer to heal than most of us realize. When we throw out moral standards and follow the free-sex philosophy, we will suffer the consequences. Like blind following blind, we will both fall in the ditch and bruise ourselves in the process. Listen to the following horror stories and look at their scars.

The scar of guilt:

I feel so dirty and empty; like a discarded beer can. He grabbed me in his arms as if he'd never let go. Our love for each other seemed as though it would never end. But then when I gave him all that I had to give, he crumpled me up in his hands and threw me away. I never thought it would happen to me. I feel like a slut.

Melinda
Seattle, Washington

The scar of rejection:

He promised me we'd get married. Then all he wanted to do was have sex every day. Once I took my foot off the brakes, he wouldn't slow down. He didn't want to play tennis. He didn't want to go swimming. He didn't want to do anything with our other friends. All he wanted was my body, and when I told him he couldn't have it anymore, he told me I was selfish and then broke up.

Susan
Tulsa, Oklahoma

The scar of depression:

Everything started going wrong. We spent all our time by ourselves. My grades went downhill. My other friends seemed to forget about me. At home I couldn't talk to my parents. They would always ask the same questions and I got tired of lying to them so I decided to just avoid them. Now I have no one to talk with about my problems and my girlfriend told me to take a hike.

George
Tampa, Florida

The scar of suspicion:
All of a sudden I realized what a fool I've been. If
he would have sex with me outside of the marriage
commitment, what is keeping him from having sex
with someone else? I realized I didn't trust him.
Since we have been married, he travels a lot. How do
I know I can trust him when he is in another city on
business? I can tell he gets terribly jealous of me too.
I can't even talk to a guy in the grocery store
without him getting furious.

Brenda
Charlotte, North Carolina

The scar of fear:
Every month I used to get so scared that I might
get pregnant. My parents would just kill me. Now I
wonder about venereal disease or AIDS. I mean,
they say you won't know if you've got it for five years
or more. It is one thing to get open sores on your
body that don't heal, but I sure don't want to die!

Vickie
Spokane, Washington

The scar of anger:
I used to have a great relationship with her but
lately we fight over everything. To tell you the
truth, it started to go downhill soon after we began
having sex. We had been dating for over a year and
all our friends were sexually active so we figured,
why not? Now we can't even get along with each
other. We expected sex to deepen our relationship,
but it almost seems to have destroyed it.

Jack
El Paso, Texas

The scar of flashbacks:
We had sex before we were married because we
figured we would get married anyway. That was
stupid. Since we were getting married anyway, why
didn't we just wait? Whenever we have sex now I
still feel dirty. I can't get it out of my mind. I know
that she did it with other guys and she knows I did

it with other girls before we were married—I can't
help but think about those other times. The whole
thing hangs over me like a cloud.

Jimmy
Tucson, Arizona

Each of these case studies gives twentieth-century evidence
that we can't break God's moral law without paying the price.
Morals may or may not be popular but they are still relevant.
God is not out to steal our joy or to take the fun out of life. He
is trying to take the sting out of life. His standards are logical,
loving limitations. He wants to save us from the bondage of
guilt, rejection, depression, suspicion, fear, anger, and jealous
flashbacks of immorality.

It is time to rediscover God's moral values. Our survival
depends upon it.

My First Date

The time to put up standards is during construction, not
after the building is completed. The time to establish a moral
standard is before we begin dating.

I will never forget my first date. What a disaster! I had not
yet established a moral standard, and it almost destroyed me.

I was in junior high when a girl three years older asked me
to a dance at her high school. I was flattered. After much
ragging, my parents gave me their permission. I was floored!

I did not yet have my driver's license, so her older brother
drove. From the moment I got into the car, I knew I had made
a big mistake. I felt like a steer on the way to slaughter.

As I sat in the backseat, she sat so close she was almost
sitting on my lap. I have seen people sit close before, but this
was ridiculous. "Are we picking up some of your friends?" I
innocently asked.

"Nope, just the two of us," she answered with an overly
aggressive look on her face.

If she had worn any more perfume, I wouldn't have been able
to breathe. I don't like cologne to begin with but hers was so
strong it smelled like insect repellent.

If she had worn any more makeup, I wouldn't have recognized her. Her eyes had so much shadow on them that she looked like Sugar Ray Leonard's sparring partner. Her eyelashes were so long, they looked like spiders. It was almost scary. Her cheeks were so encrusted with rouge and powder, they looked as if she had been hit in the face with a cake and she just let it harden.

As we drove to the high school, I didn't say a word out loud but to myself I was thinking, *Man, what a mess you got yourself into. I can't wait until this car takes me home.*

Her hair was so full of spray it felt as if she was wearing a steel-wool wig. Since I was almost twelve inches taller than she, it kept hitting me in the face. It was like barbed wire.

Her dress had such a plunging neckline, I thought for sure she had the thing on backwards. Fortunately she wore a shawl but I kept wishing even the shawl had a zipper. I almost offered her my turtleneck.

The real clincher came when we drove up to the school and got out of the car. She took me by the hand, led me through the front door, and past the gymnasium where everyone else was going. We walked so far down a dimly lit corridor, I could barely hear the band playing any longer. Finally I said, "Hey, it's not that I'm afraid of the dark, but where are we going? I mean everyone else is back there," pointing over my shoulder.

She just looked up at me, smirked, pulled me a little closer, and kept walking. *It's all over,* I said to myself. *This is all happening too fast. I'm too young to die.* She was smiling, and I was scared stiff.

I don't know what she's got in mind, but somehow I've got to get out of here. I panicked. Suddenly, an idea dawned on me. "Where's the bathroom?" I asked. I took a lengthy pit stop. I think it must have been forty-five minutes. When I finally emerged, I took one look at her face and I knew we were on different wavelengths. I felt as though I just took a seventh-inning stretch, and she looked as if the game hadn't even started. All I could do was turn around and walk back into the men's room. That place was like an air-raid shelter.

Finally, when I emerged the next time, she seemed different. "You don't feel good, do you?" she asked. She obviously thought

I had an intestinal problem. By this time I really didn't care what she thought. Anything was better than feeling like a hunted animal.

She agreed to listen to the music with everyone else. After a while, she called her brother and before long we were on our way home. I was never so glad to pull into my driveway in my life.

What was wrong with the evening? Was the girl such a creep? Not really. Was I such a goody-goody? Probably not. The problem was I had no idea what was happening. I can chuckle over the experience today, but at the time, I wasn't sure I would even survive. I had no idea where to draw the line, how to draw the line, or even why I should draw the line. All I knew was that I wanted out!

Many of us have gotten involved in dating the hard way, almost like learning to swim by being thrown into a tank full of hungry sharks. Before we realize what we are dealing with, we are under attack.

Fortunately I escaped my first date with only a few emotional bumps and bruises. I had yet to discover moral values, but at least I was spared serious injury.

Dating is not the place to get caught in the squeeze and pressured to do things we know are wrong. There is too much to lose. It is time to stand up and smash the vice vise which has a stranglehold on our generation. It is time to wake up and flee from the vicious jaws of moral compromise. It is time to dare to date differently.

We need to reestablish a strict moral standard. Let's see how, in the next chapter.

For Discussion

1. In your own words, define *moral standard*.

2. In your own words, define *values*.

3. Have you ever gotten into a "sour-milk relationship"?
   Describe what it was like.
   How did you get out?

4. Circle the scars of premarital sex you have either seen in
   someone else or experienced yourself.
   • The scar of guilt
   • The scar of rejection
   • The scar of depression
   • The scar of suspicion
   • The scar of fear
   • The scar of anger
   • The scar of flashbacks

5. Describe your first date.
   Did anything funny happen?
   How did you feel before you went out?
   How did you feel afterward?

6. Have you ever been on a date on which you felt pressured
   to become sexually involved when you didn't want to?
   What did you do about it?
   How did it make you feel?
   Is there anything you can do to avoid situations like
   that?

7. Why is it hard to "just say no"?

8. Do you tell your parents your problems?
   Why or why not?
   How do they (would they) respond?

Four

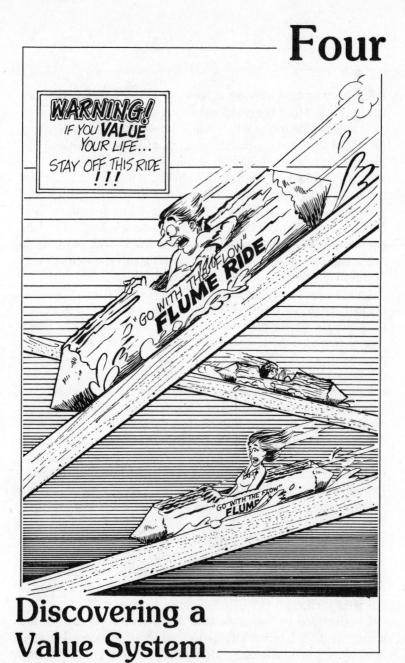

Discovering a
Value System

Jim was a fun-loving seventeen-year-old who had fallen in love for the first time. He was swept off his feet, and he acted as if no one else in the whole world knew what he was feeling. Most of his friends were cheering him on because they had never seen him so excited about anything.

"Jim," I asked, "have you established a moral standard you refuse to compromise even if it means losing your girlfriend?"

He looked back at me as if I had asked him to jump off the Empire State Building. "You've got to be kidding!" Then he explained, "My old youth pastor told me it was okay to do anything on a date as long as you didn't go all the way . . . that God doesn't give any other standards."

I had heard this idea before, so I didn't let it throw me. I just opened the Bible and handed it to him, pointing to Matthew 5:27, 28. He slowly read the verses out loud, "You have heard that it was said, 'Do not commit adultery.' But I tell you that anyone who looks at a woman lustfully has already committed adultery with her in his heart."

"The people who lived in Jesus' day had the same misunderstanding," I commented. "They thought God condemned premarital intercourse but had nothing to say about all the rest. Jesus pointed out to them that the seventh commandment not only deals with the act of premarital intercourse but it also includes all forms of passionate activity outside of marriage. It includes everything that arouses lust such as touching the private parts of another person's body or even looking lustfully."

Fortunately, Jim was a good friend, so he listened to the correction I was giving him, but it wasn't easy. "Man, you have no idea how hard this is to swallow. I have never dated a girl before. Now I have a girlfriend who really likes me . . . what if she gets turned off by some new moral standard?"

I understood the struggle that Jim was having, but to my amazement, before we left he agreed to eliminate all lustful activity in his relationship. He was afraid to tell his girlfriend but when he did, rather than rejecting him, she was impressed. "Jim, I always wanted to date a guy with moral convictions but I thought it was impossible in today's world. You are the first guy I have ever dated," she told him, "who has ever had the guts to say *no*. Jim, I sure respect you and I am grateful that you respect me, too."

The next time Jim saw me he was more excited than ever. Jim learned that setting a standard doesn't ruin a relationship. In fact, it actually protects it. Jim is a pacesetter.

A Fuzzy Gray Line

Jim expressed a popular view of morals. It sounds something like this:

> God does not tell us how far we can go. Oh, sure, there is the black area of premarital intercourse that is certainly wrong. And there is the white area of holding hands, putting our arms around each other, and a single kiss on the cheek which are certainly okay. But in the middle there is a wide range of gray— things like taking off our clothes, fondling each other's private parts, and passionate kissing—which we need to decide for ourselves when the situation presents itself. The gray is somewhere between right and wrong. It is a little wrong but it's also a little right, and since it's only normal, it is okay.

This theory of moral standards is popular, but it is dead wrong. In fact, this principle has destroyed more young men and women than all the whorehouses in history.

The only way you get the color gray is to mix white and black together. This means that moral issues which are gray are at least partially evil and we should therefore have the integrity and self-control to say no.

> *Morality* is a life-style based on God's moral standard.
> *Immorality* is a life-style in violation of God's moral standard.
> *Amorality* is a life-style that denies the existence of such a moral standard.

It is one thing for an atheist to believe there is no such thing
as a value system, but it is absurd for a Christian to suggest
such a thing. We do not need to live in a world of gray. God has
a very definite black-and-white standard of right and wrong.
Because He created us and does not want us to suffer all the
abuse, He has established a moral law that gives us the
protection we need.

God's Moral Standard

In contrast to man's fuzzy gray line, God draws a straight
line. He has never been afraid to call a sin a sin. Since sex and
love and dating and morals are all such important areas of our
lives, God doesn't leave it up to guesswork.

Let's allow the Bible to speak for itself. (You might want to
look up these verses and underline them in your own Bible.)

> Flee from sexual immorality. All other sins a man com-
> mits are outside his body, but he who sins sexually sins
> against his own body. Do you not know that your body is
> a temple of the Holy Spirit, who is in you, whom you have
> received from God? You are not your own; you were
> bought at a price. Therefore honor God with your body.
> 1 Corinthians 6:18–20

> So I say, live by the Spirit, and you will not gratify the
> desires of the sinful nature. For the sinful nature desires
> what is contrary to the Spirit, and the Spirit what is
> contrary to the sinful nature. They are in conflict with
> each other, so that you do not do what you want. But if
> you are led by the Spirit, you are not under law. The acts
> of the sinful nature are obvious: sexual immorality,
> impurity and debauchery; idolatry and witchcraft; hatred,
> discord, jealousy, fits of rage, selfish ambition, dissen-
> sions, factions and envy; drunkenness, orgies, and the
> like. I warn you, as I did before, that those who live like
> this will not inherit the kingdom of God.
> Galatians 5:16–21

> It is God's will that you should be sanctified: that you
> should avoid sexual immorality; that each of you should
> learn to control his own body in a way that is holy and

honorable, not in passionate lust like the heathen, who do
not know God; and that in this matter no one should wrong
his brother or take advantage of him. The Lord will punish
men for all such sins, as we have already told you and
warned you. For God did not call us to be impure, but to live
a holy life. Therefore, he who rejects this instruction does
not reject man but God, who gives you his Holy Spirit.

1 Thessalonians 4:3–8

Do you not know that the wicked will not inherit the
kingdom of God? Do not be deceived: Neither the sexually
immoral nor idolaters nor adulterers nor male prostitutes
nor homosexual offenders nor thieves nor the greedy nor
drunkards nor slanderers nor swindlers will inherit the
kingdom of God.

1 Corinthians 6:9, 10

"You have heard that it was said, 'Do not commit
adultery.' But I tell you that anyone who looks at a
woman lustfully has already committed adultery with
her in his heart. If your right eye causes you to sin,
gouge it out and throw it away. It is better for you to lose
one part of your body than for your whole body to be
thrown into hell."

Matthew 5:27–29

. . . I will walk in my house with blameless heart. I will
set before my eyes no vile thing.

Psalms 101:2, 3

"I made a covenant with my eyes not to look lustfully at
a girl."

Job 31:1

But among you there must not be even a hint of sexual
immorality, or of any kind of impurity, or of greed,
because these are improper for God's holy people. Nor
should there be obscenity, foolish talk or coarse joking,
which are out of place, but rather thanksgiving. For of
this you can be sure: No immoral, impure or greedy

person—such a man is an idolater—has any inheritance
in the kingdom of Christ and of God.

Ephesians 5:3–5

Flee the evil desires of youth, and pursue righteousness,
faith, love and peace, along with those who call on the
Lord out of a pure heart.

2 Timothy 2:22

Then I heard another voice from heaven say: "Come out of
her, my people, so that you will not share in her sins, so
that you will not receive any of her plagues; for her sins
are piled up to heaven, and God has remembered her
crimes."

Revelation 18:4, 5

"Blessed are those who wash their robes, that they may
have the right to the tree of life and may go through the
gates into the city. Outside are the dogs, those who
practice magic arts, the sexually immoral, the murderers,
the idolaters and everyone who loves and practices
falsehood."

Revelation 22:14, 15

"Enter through the narrow gate. For wide is the gate and
broad is the road that leads to destruction, and many
enter through it. But small is the gate and narrow the
road that leads to life, and only a few find it."

Matthew 7:13, 14

Do not be deceived: God cannot be mocked. A man reaps
what he sows. The one who sows to please his sinful
nature, from that nature will reap destruction; the one
who sows to please the Spirit from the Spirit will reap
eternal life.

Galatians 6:7, 8

How can a young man keep his way pure? By living
according to your word. . . I have hidden your word in my
heart that I might not sin against you.

Psalms 119:9, 11

God's moral standard is the only moral standard we need. Even in a day when our generation is running blindly as if no such standard existed, we need to stand up and make it our own. As a missionary friend of mine, Elaine Battles, once said, "Any ol' dead fish can float downstream!" It takes a live, energetic young person to swim against the flow.

No Dead Fish

God's moral standard is *no lust*. Not only does Jesus declare sexual intercourse outside of marriage off limits, but He also bans even looking lustfully. As the Apostle Paul wrote to his healthy young friend Timothy, "Flee youthful lusts" (*see* 2 Timothy 2:22).

Since lust is off limits, we obviously need to eliminate passionate kissing, undressing and fondling each other's private parts. If lustful looking is forbidden, lustful touching is certainly forbidden.

You show me anyone who can stroke another's private parts, undress a date, or even engage in heavy kissing without arousing lustful desire, and I'll show you a dead fish. Unless you are dead or almost dead, it is impossible. Therefore all such activities are ruled off limits according to God's standards.

God made for us a list of what He considers dead-fish activities: "The acts of the sinful nature are obvious: sexual immorality, impurity and debauchery; idolatry and witchcraft; hatred, discord, jealousy, fits of rage, selfish ambition, dissensions, factions and envy; drunkenness, orgies, and the like. I warn you, as I did before, that those who live like this will not inherit the kingdom of God. . . . Those who belong to Christ Jesus have crucified the sinful nature with its passions and desires" (Galatians 5:19–21, 24).

Let's consider what some of these words mean.

Sexual immorality is translated from the Greek word *porneia* from which we get the word *pornography*. It is usually translated "fornication" or "premarital intercourse" but also refers to other sensuous activities that lead up to intercourse. God says off limits.

Impurity is also translated "uncleanness." It refers to anything we consider dirty—dirty movies, dirty magazines, dirty jokes, dirty conversation, dirty books. The Bible tells us to be "hating even the garment spotted by the flesh" (Jude 23 RSV). God looks at all this dirty stuff and says off limits!

Debauchery is usually translated "licentiousness" and it literally means "that which arouses lustful desires" or "following an inclination toward sensuality." Since avoiding debauchery is part of God's standard, we also need to make it our own standard. We need to say, "I will not be involved in the dead-fish activity which arouses lustful desires or that follows an inclination toward sensuality."

God lovingly tells us as His children, "Among you there must not be even a hint of sexual immorality, or of any kind of impurity, or of greed, because these are improper for God's holy people" (Ephesians 5:3).

Liberty

There is a whole new breed of young person committed to the life-style of moral purity. If sexual activity outside of marriage brings bondage, fleeing such activity brings a wonderful freedom. Listen to these exciting accounts I have received from those pacesetters who are committed to living according to God's standard no matter what the cost.

The badge of self-respect:
I have never been so happy in my life. I am finally dating a Christian guy who has the same moral standards I have. We don't mess around at all, and it is wonderful. We both have the goal of putting Jesus first, and I have never felt so good about myself.

                                                    Barbara
                                        Grand Rapids, Michigan

The badge of creativity:
My girlfriend and I both agree not to mess around sexually before marriage. Since we have been dat-

ing, I have been doing better in school. I feel I have
direction in life. I am not wasting my creative juices
on lustful activity. I can channel all my energies
toward constructive projects.

Tommy
Birmingham, Alabama

The badge of kindness:
I have never dated a guy like this before. Rather
than wanting to spend all our time off by ourselves,
we do all kinds of neat things to help other people.
Every Sunday afternoon we visit the nursing home
and talk to elderly people. Tuesday evenings we lead
a Bible club with my little sister and her neighborhood friends.

Gloria
Topeka, Kansas

The badge of stamina:
We play tennis together, ride bikes, and even jog a
couple times a week. I have never been in such great
shape. Since I've learned to control my sexual desires, it has helped me diet and exercise properly.

Sam
Portland, Maine

The badge of peace:
We really respect each other. I know that she
cares about who I am and she knows that I feel the
same way about her. Neither of us gets jealous even
though we won't see each other for the whole summer. We have both given our relationship to Jesus
and are trusting Him to take care of it. Since we
don't mess around with each other, I guess we have
no reason to suspect our standards to change when
we are separate.

Gordon
Denver, Colorado

The badge of a clear conscience:
Last night before we hung up he told me that I am
the first girl who encourages him to be all that God

wants him to be. That made me feel really good
inside. I know I feel the same way about him. Even
my parents have noticed a change in my life. I don't
need to hide anything from them anymore. . . . We
sit up all hours of the night talking. It's excellent!

Mari
Princeton, New Jersey

The badge of joy:
I have dated a lot of people but I have never before
done it God's way. I still have a lot to learn but at
least I have learned the basics. I have established a
moral standard that I refuse to compromise and so
has my girlfriend. The thing we can't believe is how
happy we are. It really feels good to be clean inside
and clean towards God. My friends sometimes think
I'm crazy but they still admit that I seem to be
enjoying myself. I wish more of my friends could
know how great it is to be morally straight.

Len
Harrisburg, Pennsylvania

Committing yourself to a strict moral standard might seem
like locking yourself up in a monastery and throwing away the
key. Actually, as we have seen from all these twentieth-
century examples, the opposite is true. To play around with sex
before marriage is to become a prisoner to moral bondage. But
to set a standard and stick to it without compromise is to enjoy
moral freedom. True freedom is not the right to do what we
want, but the power to do what we ought.

As the Bible says, "It is for freedom that Christ has set us
free. Stand firm, then, and do not let yourselves be burdened
again by a yoke of slavery" (Galatians 5:1).

Positive Pacesetters

It is pathetic that in the middle of a generation crying out for
someone to stand up and show them an alternative to the
free-sex fantasy, many of us have quietly dropped out. Our
generation does not need some self-righteous soapbox preacher

to stand up in P.E. class and arrogantly tell everyone else they need to shape up. What our generation needs is a few of us to begin living according to the standard we claim to believe. This is no time to quit the race. Now is the time to literally become pacesetters on our campuses and among our friends. Whether we realize it or not, our friends are looking for someone to stand up and say, "Here is another life-style. I have found it fun and freeing and exciting!"

World evangelist Billy Graham said, "I find that youth want moral guidelines. They want to be told with authority what is right and what is wrong."

Fortunately, God has given us an authority of right and wrong in the Bible. We have the truth which can serve as an antidote to the moral disease among our peers. Are we willing to live it first and then share it with others? There are plenty of dead fish who are floating downriver. It is time to swim against the flow. It is time to make God's moral standard our moral standard. It is time to dare to date differently.

For Discussion

1. If you established a strict moral standard that you
   refused to compromise even if it meant losing dates,
   how do you think your friends would respond? How
   would your boyfriend or girlfriend respond?

2. Are you willing to establish a strict moral standard?
   Why or why not?

3. Do you know anyone who has established a strict moral
   standard?
   What do you think of that person?
   How do friends treat that person?

4. What hinders more people from establishing such a
   moral standard?

5. Describe in your own words "the fuzzy gray line" view
   of sexual morals.
   Have you ever heard of this theory before reading about
   it in this chapter?

6. Define the terms *morality, immorality,* and *amorality.*

7. Which Bible verses in this chapter help us understand
   how God answers the question, "How far can we go?"

8. What does "Any ol' dead fish can float downstream"
   mean?

9. Which benefits of dating with a strict moral standard do you desire to see in your own life? Circle them.
   • Badge of self-respect
   • Badge of creativity
   • Badge of kindness
   • Badge of stamina
   • Badge of peace
   • Badge of a clear conscience
   • Badge of joy

10. What does the author mean by *pacesetters*?

five

Moral Pacesetters

Once we establish a strict moral standard based on God's standard of *no lust,* we become candidates for moral leadership in our generation.

I want to introduce you to a special girl. Her name is Kelly. I met her four years ago at a teen camp in Florida. One night as I was walking back to my cabin, I spotted her sitting on a tree stump all by herself. She was sobbing.

"You want to talk?" I gently asked.

She looked startled, wiped away some tears, and said with a candid half-smile, "I think I need to talk." She spilled her guts. She told me about her parents' divorce, living with her mother, being the youngest in the family, and the only kid still living at home. "She lets me do anything I want. It's not that she trusts me . . . she just doesn't seem to care. This past year I messed up bad. I was going with a guy, and we slept together. I knew it was wrong and now that I gave my life to Jesus tonight, I feel even worse. I feel like I really let Him down." She cried again.

I opened my Bible and showed Kelly what Jesus told the woman caught in adultery (John 8:1–11). "Kelly, first of all Jesus said, *I do not condemn you.* She felt guilty because she was guilty. But Jesus forgave her. He forgives you too." I looked at her to see if it was sinking in. "Isn't that good news, Kelly? That He forgives us?" She nodded. "Now if Jesus doesn't condemn us, we must not condemn ourselves either.

"Then Jesus said to the woman, *Go and sin no more.* He not only wiped her slate clean, He told her to keep it that way. He gave her a new start and He also gave her a new moral standard. Kelly, He wants to give you, not only a new start, but a new moral standard also. It's not too late. You're not an old maid or some leftover. He loves you, and He will take good care of you." By now she was smiling. "In fact, Jesus said, *I make all things new.* He can do that for you."

I could tell she was getting excited when she asked me, "Where do I start?" We looked at what the Bible says about our

moral standard of no lust. I warned her, "Now that you have
already messed up sexually, you have a weakness. You need to
fortify yourself against further failure by memorizing many of
these verses and you need to hold to the strict moral standard
even if it means losing dates."

I knew she accepted the challenge when she stood up, dusted
herself off, looked me square in the eye, stretched out her hand
to me, and said, "Well, you better pray for me!"

"It's a deal," I agreed as I shook her hand.

I meet many teenagers all over the country, but that night
Kelly made a lasting impression. She accepted the high challenge, and I felt a strong desire to pray for her.

Last year I had a rewarding experience. I spoke at a
Christian college and after the meeting guess who ran up and
gave me a bear hug? You guessed it! Kelly.

"You'd be proud of me!" she said with a big grin. She
introduced me to many of her friends who told me much about
Kelly. They told me about her being in school band, cheerlead-
ing and the homecoming court. I took them out for pizza that
night. They admitted that when they first met her they
thought she was too puritanical—too straight. They admitted
to mocking her, but they were amazed that the teasing didn't
seem to faze her.

"She was still the same Kelly. She still joked around with us.
Even when we were hard on her, we could tell she still loved us.
Kelly is a strong person. Everyone on campus respects her
moral values. She's taught us a lot."

Kelly is a new breed. She is a model, a leader, a pacesetter.
Besides following the rules, as far as her friends are concerned,
she wrote the rules. She committed herself to follow Jesus
down the righteous highway when everyone else was stuck in
the mud. Even though she failed morally in high school, she
purposed to win in college and she did.

Last week I received a letter from Kelly: "Guess what? I'm
getting married. I'm so excited. My fiancé loves the Lord and is
preparing to be a minister. He is just as committed to maintaining a strict moral standard as I am. Are you still praying
for me?"

Kelly is now experiencing the reward of moral freedom. God gave her a fresh, clean start, and she made the most of it.

My heart cries out to God, "O Lord, raise up a new generation of Kellys. On every campus across the land, raise up young men and women who will take a stand for You. Call out a new breed of young people who will dare to date differently."

Reactions

It has been my experience that once we commit ourselves to a definite moral standard and refuse to compromise even if it means losing dates, we will experience a series of reactions from people around us.

Reaction #1: Friends will look at us in amazement and say to themselves, *What got into him? He can't be for real.* Or, *Who does she think she is?*

Reaction #2: They will poke us, slap us, maybe even bite into us, chew us up and spit us out. This is usually done to see what we're really made of. They want to see if we are faking it or if we are for real.

Reaction #3: If we survive phase two, we will usually win their respect and our life-style will then become an alternative for them to consider. If we compromise and give in to the pressure, we will win their disrespect and we will always be remembered as the yo-yo—full of moral ups and downs.

Reaction #4: Once we have held our ground, refusing to compromise and have won their respect, we have now graduated to the level of pacesetter, model, moral leader. We personally become a standard for others. Our life-style becomes an alternative which some of our friends will actually imitate. Sure, there will always be opposition, but the exciting part is that we are playing a significant part in reforming an adulterous generation. We are on the cutting edge where all the action is.

The only way to make a difference is to dare to be different. If I choose to just fit in and go along with the crowd, my life won't amount to any more than a beef jerky. When people think of me, their only reaction will be to yawn. If I want to be a leader, if I want to help shape my generation, then I must be willing to live differently. I can't be afraid of making waves.

If we start dating differently, it will be like dancing to the beat of a different drum. At first some people will probably laugh. After a while, the band might stop playing, and they might even try to kick us off the dance floor. But if we keep dancing, it won't take long until people around us start to realize that we know something they don't know. They will, for perhaps the first time, realize there is another way to dance.

A New Year's Eve Party

When I was in twelfth grade I established a moral standard based on the Bible. My old friends invited me to a New Year's Eve party. I knew it would be wild because along with the invitation to the party I received an order form for as much beer, wine, and marijuana as I wanted. My old friends were messed up but they certainly were well organized.

I asked my parents if I could go, and they left the decision up to me. "You have earned the responsibility to make your own decision. You pray about it and we'll pray for you."

I knew I would face much pressure, and it would be a little like swimming in front of a gigantic jewfish, but surprisingly I felt as though I should go. Besides my parents, I also recruited my minister and my youth minister to pray for me.

That night as I drove up, cars were parked all the way down the street. The music was so loud I could hear it three blocks away. When I walked inside the house the smoke was so thick, the visibility was not much more than three feet. I must admit I felt out of place . . . even a little scared.

A girl whom I hadn't seen for five years came up to me. We talked for a while. Then she put her arms around my neck, kissed my cheek, and whispered, "You wanna go upstairs?"

Just to let you know the frame of mind I was in, I innocently asked, "What for?"

She smiled and pulled my head a little closer and again whispered, "To go to bed."

I knew I would be tested, but I sure never thought it would

come right out and grab me around the neck like that. But I was ready. I stepped back, squared my shoulders, looked her right in the eye and said, "I would love to go to bed with you except I'm a Christian and my body belongs to Jesus. I don't intend to do that until I'm married and then I'm sure it will be wonderful." I could hardly believe what I had said. The words just flowed out of my mouth. She looked back at me as if I had turned into a werewolf or some creature from the deep lagoon. I really didn't care. In fact, inside I felt good because I knew I had passed the test.

There was just one problem. I spoke too loud. At least a dozen heads turned to look at me. Their mouths hung open. The poor girl felt like crawling out the window.

"Well, I guess the party is over," I said as I looked around the room. "So if it's okay with you I'd like to tell you how Jesus has changed my life." For the next half hour I shared my story with my old friends, and I was able to explain to them what Jesus had done in my life. I have never seen such an attentive group. They were not sure how to respond but no one laughed, no one even got up and left. In fact, a couple of old friends came up to me and told me they had never heard anything like that before. Two weeks later, one of my old friends even asked Jesus to come into his life. That's exciting.

Ownership

If we are going to date differently, there is a simple ten-word sentence we need to learn: *My body belongs to Jesus, and I don't do that*. We need to use this sentence when someone offers us a marijuana cigarette and we need to use it when our boyfriend or girlfriend wants to pull our pants down.

Needless to say, every time we feel pressure to lower our standards, it will not be as dramatic as the New Year's Eve party was for me. The right words will not always come out of our mouths. At times we will stutter like fools. We will not always win the respect of our friends. At times they will walk away laughing at us. That is all part of daring to date differently. To a generation caught in moral quicksand, anyone who climbs out will seem like a deserter. But unless some of us climb out first, no one will survive. Our generation desperately needs moral pacesetters.

My friend Kelly became a pacesetter at college. But if she had not felt forgiven she would never have been even able to start the race. She would still be in the starting blocks.

Most of us have done things we know were wrong. We have messed up and unless we deal with our guilt we are not going anywhere. Let's find out more about forgiveness, in the next chapter.

For Discussion

1. Have you ever known a girl (or guy) like Kelly, who
   became morally strong?
   Tell that person's story.

2. Why do we all admire people like Kelly?

3. The author says, "The only way to make a difference in
   our generation is to dare to be different."
   Explain.
   Do you agree or disagree?

4. What reaction does the crowd have when someone starts
   living according to a new value system?
   How do the reactions change after a while?

5. Have you ever been to a party like the New Year's Eve
   party the author described?
   Explain.
   How did you feel?
   Did you fit in?

6. When we hold to a moral standard, the author recom-
   mends saying, "My body belongs to Jesus. . . ."
   Why does he recommend this?
   What effect is that statement supposed to have?   ,

7. On what do most people base their moral standards?

8. Describe the moral standard of some popular kid in your
   school.

9. Describe your moral standard.
   On what is your moral standard based?

six

I Forgive You

Every time I speak on the subject of sex, morals, and dating, there are always young people who feel deeply guilty. They are overwhelmed with regrets.

A few years ago I spoke to a group of twenty high-school students. After my talk, a girl came up to me with her head down and tears running off her cheeks. She was shaking. She couldn't look at me, but she quietly asked if we could go outside and talk.

"I can't take it any longer," she started. "I haven't told this to anyone. I've been so afraid. I know you're going to think I'm a slut," she cried.

"It's okay," I assured her.

"Last spring I started dating this guy named Tony. One night we went out into a field, and he got me drunk. Then he talked me into taking off my clothes," she sobbed. "It hurt so bad. We had sex. I felt so cheap. And then after that night, he never spoke to me again. I just hate him. And I hate myself."

We talked for a while. I read her some verses in the Bible. Later another girl came up to me and motioned that she wanted to talk privately.

"Last spring I started dating this guy Tony. One night he got me out in a field. We drank wine. He took off my clothes. I didn't really know what was going on. We had sex but I was drunk and I barely remember what happened. It was gross. I feel so guilty from it. At times I wish I was dead. I wouldn't dare tell my parents. In fact, I've never told anyone about this. Is there any way I can feel clean again?"

We talked. I read her verses from the Bible. She seemed assured of God's love for her. Then a third girl came up to me with tears rolling down her face. She wanted to talk alone.

"I'm embarrassed to talk about this, but I have to. I feel sick to my stomach. I've never told anyone before but I think I can trust you. Anyway, last spring this guy from my school named Tony got me drunk. He took me out in a field, we took off our clothes and had sex. It happened so fast. It was nothing like what I expected. I felt used. I gave him everything and he didn't even care." She wept deeply.

We talked. I read her the Bible verses also and she seemed encouraged. Since I told them I would keep their names secret, I did not tell them about one another. But it was easy for me to see that it was the same guy—Tony—who used the same scheme to trick three nice girls into having sex with him in the same field. What a bummer! These three girls were friends. They went to the same high school, were in many of the same classes, and they attended the same church. Yet they each fell for the same trick without knowing anything about the others. All three girls lost their virginity within a few months because each let down her guard. As far as I know, to this day none of the girls has shared with the others. They each came to me in need of the same thing. They each needed to hear Jesus say to them, "I forgive you."

Guilt Feelings

Have you ever done something that made you feel so guilty you questioned whether God still loved you? Have you ever said, "God can forgive anything but He can't forgive me for *that!*"?

Guilt makes God's face look mean and angry. In fact, psychologists tell us it is impossible to develop an intimate relationship with anyone who makes us feel guilty. When we have strong feelings of guilt floating around inside, our relationship with Jesus isn't going anywhere. Whenever we start to run with Jesus, our guilt feelings are like handles the devil grabs onto and pulls us backwards screaming, "You phony! You can't follow Jesus in the shape you're in. You are a loser. Crawl back in your hole." We shrug our shoulders, throw our hands up in the air, and assume there is no escape.

Suicide

The headlines read, PREGNANT TEEN TAKES HER OWN LIFE. The article told of a fourteen-year-old girl, Melody (name changed), who was nine months pregnant and apparently couldn't handle the guilt. She was a pretty girl, an average student, and well-liked by her friends. She attended a Baptist church every week, where she had been baptized.

Melody wrote in her notebook, "I ran away from all of my problems. I am taking the easy way out. I am admitting to myself that I am a weak person, not able to handle the weight of life." She tried to deny being pregnant but everyone knew. It became very obvious.

The day Melody died she opened her spiral notebook. "To my dear Mom," she began and then filled three pages. "I am very sorry to put you through all the trouble. I think everything I have to do is done. I drank some wine and took some pills. But before I did all that, I prayed to my Father God in heaven. I asked Him to forgive me, but He won't. I don't blame Him for that. Please pray that I won't be sent to hell because then I won't be able to come back and watch over you and help you. I want to do that. Mom, please don't have a nervous breakdown and be crying all the time. I don't want you to. I want you to live forever and ever, the way you want to and I will always love you very much. Please try and forgive me. I love you always and always. Love, Melody."

Melody ran on the railroad tracks two miles from school, knelt down, clasped her hands in prayer. The Amtrak train traveling one hundred miles an hour slammed on its brakes, but it was too late. The train engineer saw Melody cross herself and then . . . Melody and her unborn baby boy died instantly.

Melody is one genuine example of a teenage pregnancy and the guilt feelings that follow. There are literally thousands of girls who stand in at least part of her shadow. Many have said with Melody, "I asked Him to forgive me, but He won't."

My heart weeps for Melody and for all the young men and women across our country who have made similar wrong decisions and are filled with regret. Right now I wish I could sit down next to you, put my arm around your shoulder, look you right in the eye and say, "I have good news for you. There is nothing you have done that can drain the reservoir of God's love."

When we have sex outside of marriage, we are wrong. But

when we say, "I asked Him to forgive me, but He won't," we are also wrong. In fact, the second wrong is worse than the first.

Fake Confession

Confession is different from spilling the beans in public or hanging out our dirty laundry. Celebrities have struck it rich writing their true confessions in best-selling books. They tell of sexual encounters right down to the very last gory détail. They couldn't care less about forgiveness. They just want to sell books and receive fat royalty checks.

Confession is different from sitting in a psychiatrist's office, digging through our memory banks. We might dig up some dirt and uncover some guilt feelings but we don't want forgiveness. We simply want to feel better.

Confession is different from sitting in a booth privately talking to a priest or minister about our sins and shortcomings. Too many of my friends have said to me less than ten minutes after such a session, "Good, I got that over with. Now I'm all set until next Saturday night." Such confession is not seeking forgiveness. Such confession is almost seeking permission to go sin again. It is almost like saying, "I got away with it last time. Next time it shouldn't be any problem either."

True Confession

Confession not only admits that I was wrong but it also admits that God was right in condemning my wrong actions. The Greek word for "confess" is *homologeo* which literally means, "to say the same thing, to repeat, or to agree with." Confession says, "God, You are right in saying I was wrong." In a phrase, confession pleads "guilty as charged."

Confession not only wants to get rid of the guilt feeling but it also wants to get rid of the sin which caused the guilt feeling. Confession is more interested in pleasing God than pleasing itself. The fact that God is justly displeased with my life is more significant to me than the fact that I don't feel good about myself. Deep down I want God to be pleased with me, and I am

willing to change my life-style and my dating behavior in order
to please Him even if my friends don't understand.

At times a child who is told she is about to get a spanking
will run up to her daddy, throw her arms around his neck,
pretend to cry tears of repentance, only hoping that her father
will put his belt back in the loops of his trousers before he lays
it across her rear end. Hey, sometimes it works. Such a child is
not confessing or repenting. Such a child is manipulating. She
is only trying to alter the punishment without necessarily
altering her conduct.

When my daughter Andrea was four years old, she walked
up to me with an unusually somber face. Without saying a
word, she handed me a wooden spoon, took me by the hand, and
showed me the scene of the crime. She had broken a piece of
furniture because she was doing something she had already
been told not to do. She looked up at me. Her face was full of
regret. Then she bent over and waited for me to spank her.
Wow, I said to myself, *how can I hit a kid who has already
thoroughly repented?* She admitted she was wrong, and she
admitted I was right in punishing her. She was not so concerned about simply getting rid of her guilt feelings as she
earnestly wanted to get rid of her rebellious behavior.

I swallowed hard, winced, and smacked her anyway (not
very hard). She cried a little. We hugged. She thanked me for
loving her. We talked for a minute, and then we went outside
and played freeze tag.

The reason I smacked her was to teach her that repentance
is not done to remove punishment. Repentance is done to
remove sin. There are too many wimpy Christians today with
a wimpy view of confession. They want to feel better and get on
with things as usual without becoming any closer to Jesus.

The result of true confession is the assurance of forgiveness.
Forgiveness is the most precious gift God gives. It is the gift
that assures us we will live with Christ forever in heaven. It is
the gift that allows us to have peace of mind here on earth. It
is the gift that convinces us that God still loves us despite what
we've done.

Forgiveness is not something we can produce ourselves. We
can't psych ourselves up into feeling forgiven. It is not the

result of positive thinking or positive talking. It is something we must receive as a free gift from Jesus. The only way we can get it from Him is by true confession.

The Bible says, "If we confess our sins, he is faithful and just and will forgive us our sins and purify us from all unrighteousness" (1 John 1:9).

God doesn't want us to beg Him for forgiveness. He doesn't expect us to walk across cut glass or sleep in a bed of nails. God simply wants us to confess—to agree with Him that sin is sin and that He is justly displeased with it. Then let it go, renounce it, forsake it. We hold out our empty hands and receive from Jesus His precious gift of forgiveness. He won't force it on us, but we can receive it. There is nothing greater in this world than to hear Jesus quietly say, "I forgive you."

Spend thirty-five seconds thinking about the following sentence. *There is no saint without a past and no sinner without a future.*

A Clean Start

Melody is dead. She thought God was unable to forgive her and she would rather be dead than to live with her guilt. She knelt down on a railroad track, thinking that anything would be better than the pain she felt. We can understand how she felt, but I wish someone could have explained God's love to her before it was too late.

I can no longer talk with her, but I can talk with you. Do you want a clean start? Do you want to be forgiven and feel clean inside? You don't need to be dying inside from guilt and sin you have not confessed.

David, the man after God's own heart, sinned like an all-star. He was guilty of immorality, deceit, murder, and cover-up. Then he held it inside without confession, and it almost killed him. Listen to his description:

> When I kept silent,
>   my bones wasted away
>   through my groaning all day long.

For day and night
   your hand was heavy upon me;
my strength was sapped
   as in the heat of summer.
Then I acknowledged my sin to you
   and did not cover up my iniquity.
I said, "I will confess
   my transgressions to the Lord"—
and you forgave
   the guilt of my sin.
Psalms 32:3–5

God loves us and wants us to come out from hiding. He knows all about our disobedience anyway. We can't hide anything from Him.

If you have sin and guilt in your life, right now you can talk with Jesus about it. He wants you to turn your life over to Him, and He wants to say to you, "I forgive you."

Read this prayer and consider using it as your personal commitment to Jesus.

> Jesus, You know I have messed up. You know all about it. I have felt sick inside about what I did, but I want to confess it to You now.
>
> Jesus, even though I don't feel like it, the Bible tells me You love me anyway. You died on the cross to forgive my sins and to pay the debt I owed. You loved me while I was a sinner and You love me now.
>
> The Bible says if I confess my sins You will forgive me and wash me clean inside. Right now come inside and change me. Remove all the junk. Thank You for forgiving me.
>
> Wrap Your arms of love around me and protect me. From now on I want to live for You. I know I have been bought with a price and that I belong to You. Show me how I can live for You and invest my time, talents, and energy in serving You. Praise You, Lord! Amen.

For Discussion

1. When you read about the three girls who each had sex with Tony, how did you feel towards them?
   If they asked you for help, what would you say?
   How did you feel towards Tony?

2. How did you feel towards Melody, who killed herself on the train track?
   What would you have told her, if she were your friend?

3. Have you ever done anything for which you felt God couldn't forgive you?
   Have you ever had trouble forgiving yourself for anything?

4. What is worse: Having sex outside of marriage or feeling as if God can't forgive you for having sex outside of marriage?

5. Define *guilt*.
   What causes it?
   Is it good or bad?
   What effect does it have?

6. Describe *fake confession*.
   What effect does it have?

7. Describe *true confession*.
   What effect does it have?

8. Explain the statement, "There is no saint without a past and no sinner without a future."

9. When we mess up morally and do what we know is wrong, what can we do about it?

seven

X-Rated Videos

When we allow Jesus to come inside and clean our hearts, we also need to let Him clean our closets. Many of us have hidden things from our parents somewhere in our rooms. If we are serious about cleaning up our act, we need to allow Jesus to point out to us which of our secret goodies needs to get hauled off to the nearest dumpster.

Peter's Porno

Peter was only ten when he flipped through his first *Playboy* magazine. While playing hide and seek, he knocked it off the shelf in his dad's closet and the magazine opened to the middle. When he picked it up, he couldn't believe his eyes. He felt funny inside. Something said, *Hey, this is no good. You'd better hide somewhere else.* But as he put it back on the shelf, something else inside said, *Go ahead, take another peek.* His curiosity got the best of him. It became a habit. Every afternoon when he got home from school, he quietly went into his dad's closet. He found a whole stack of those magazines. The more he looked, the more interested he became. He couldn't get enough of them.

By the time Peter came to me he was twenty years old and he had all the signs of ten long years of exposure to dirty pictures. He sat in my office with his head down. I told him he could avoid the gory details, that God knew all about it and there was no need to rerun all the mistakes. As Peter told his story, his body convulsed. Everything had been built up. No one else in the world knew what he had been into. I was the first person he told, and it was almost as though he was vomiting up all the garbage he had been feeding on for years but couldn't digest.

Private Porno

Not many of us have seen as much as Peter but most of us have looked at more than we should. While growing up I looked through only three pornographic magazines, but that is three more than I wish I had.

If we think we can protect our bodies with strict moral standards while we secretly fill our minds with all sorts of sexual fantasies, we are mistaken. Those secret sexual fantasies we review like private videos do more damage than we realize. We think we will never get caught. We think our silent sin will never do us any harm. Little do we realize all the garbage we are putting into our minds is like dumping toxic waste into a reservoir. Sooner or later it will have a devastating effect.

The wise King Solomon asked two very logical questions, "Can a man carry fire to his chest without being burned? Can a man walk on hot coals without his feet getting scorched?" (*see* Proverbs 6:27, 28).

When God tells us to flee youthful lusts, He certainly includes private lusts as well as public. Again Solomon said, "As a man thinks in his heart, so is he" (*see* Proverbs 23:7). The Apostle Paul adds, "The mind set on the sinful nature is death" (*see* Romans 8:6, 7).

There are many harmful results from pornography: *Guilt,* knowing that it is wrong; *fear* over the possibility of getting caught; *dishonesty* over having to hide the magazines; *loneliness* because it is a secret we keep to ourselves.

Listen to this young woman as she tells her story in Chicago before the 1986 President's Commission on Pornography.

> I am a former Playboy bunny . . . I never questioned the morality of becoming a Playboy bunny because the magazine was accepted at home. During my time with Playboy I experienced everything from date-rape to physical abuse to group sex and finally to fantasizing homosexuality as I read Playboy magazine.
>
> I was extremely suicidal and sought psychiatric help for the eight years I lived in a sexually promiscuous fashion. There was no help for me until I changed my life-style to be a follower of Jesus Christ and obeyed the biblical truths including no premarital sex.

Public Porno

We need to understand Peter is not alone. Most teenagers have seen things and done things they later regretted.

There are close to twenty thousand porno bookstores thriving in middle-class communities all across the country. That means there are three times as many "adult" bookstores as McDonald's restaurants.

There are 20 million porno magazines printed every month. *Penthouse* alone prints four thousand every hour. Henry Boatwright, chairman of the U.S. Advisory Board of Social Concerns, estimates that 70 percent of all pornographic magazines sold eventually ends up in the hands of minors. Porno videocassettes made $150 million in 1983. MTV with its music videos dripping with violence and sex is the most popular piece of television with 21 million daily viewers compared with a meager 14 million who view Dan Rather's "CBS Evening News."

It is sick to think so much raw sex is sold dirt cheap, but it is even more disgusting to realize it is in such demand. Videos that show nudity, oral sex, group sex, homosexuality, animal sex, and kiddie sex are an abomination to God.

The Bible advises us, "For you were once darkness, but now you are light in the Lord. Live as children of light (for the fruit of the light consists in all goodness, righteousness and truth) and find out what pleases the Lord. Have nothing to do with the fruitless deeds of darkness, but rather expose them. For it is shameful even to mention what the disobedient do in secret" (Ephesians 5:8–12).

Brainwashing

Well-known rock star Barry McGuire started reading the Bible. The more he read, the more he enjoyed it. He realized the Bible was written to let people know they could have eternal life. Soon after beginning this new habit, he prayed and asked Jesus to come into his life and make him a new person. He was amazed at the change that took place and so was everyone else.

His old friends began teasing him, "Hey, you better not read the Bible so much; you're getting brainwashed."

He simply replied, "That's good. These dirty old brains need a good washing."

The Bible is the detergent that scrubs our brains clean. It says, "Do not conform any longer to the pattern of this world, but be transformed by the renewing of your mind . . ." (Romans 12:2). If we are going to be revolutionized, it needs to start in our minds.

I told my friend Peter, who had been reading pornography for ten years, "Hey, your brains might be scrambled with all the junk you've been looking at, but God's Word is powerful." I read him a verse, "The word of God is living and active. Sharper than any double-edged sword . . . it judges the thoughts and attitudes of the heart" (Hebrews 4:12).

Peter went home, dug up all his old porno magazines, took them out behind the barn, and burned them. Then he started memorizing certain verses to fortify his weakened brain. It was a radical change.

Peter has since gone to Bible college, seminary, and today he is serving his Lord as a missionary in Europe. Before he left, he called me and said, "Fred, I still think about coming to see you that day and what a change took place in my life when I gave my mind to Christ. He has salvaged my life and now it is my privilege to go serve others in need. Thanks."

A Personal Example

While a student at Wheaton College I started taking seriously my need to get "brainwashed." I wanted to clean up my thoughts and quit looking improperly at coeds on campus.

One morning while walking to class I was quoting Psalms 119:9, 11 (RSV): "How can a young man keep his way pure? By guarding it according to thy word. . . . I have laid up thy word in my heart, that I might not sin against thee."

A female form strutting down the other side of the street caught my eye. She had a set of the longest legs I had ever seen topped by one of the shortest dresses I had ever seen. *Oh, no!* I panicked. *This is a test . . . I must not fail the test.*

I fixed my gaze straight ahead, held up my Bible like a shield to obscure my vision in her direction, and walked forward full speed ahead quoting the verse out loud, *How can a young man keep his way pure? By guarding it according to thy Word.* I was safe, and I passed the test.

A few days later I was sitting in Shakespeare class. As far as I can figure out, the human brain would rather do just about anything than study Shakespeare. At least my brain would! I found myself frequently daydreaming or even dozing off. One afternoon while sitting in the back row, my mind wandered and my attention drifted to the girl sitting next to me, also hunched over her desk. The only problem was she was wearing a halter top which, from my angle, was far more revealing than I'm sure she intended.

Instantly, I snapped out of my stupor. *This is a test,* I reminded myself, and proceeded to quote my verses, *How can a young man keep his way pure?* Then I mumbled under my breath, "By guarding it according to thy Word." I thrust my Bible in the air like a shield for my own dramatic emphasis.

When I had finished my mini spiritual battle, I noticed a peculiar silence in the room. I looked up at my professor who was looking back at me through her bifocals wondering if I had had a seizure and possibly needed an ambulance. She lost her train of thought and got flustered. "It's okay, professor," I assured her, "it's just the devil being seized and my thoughts being taken captive."

The brain is an awesome mechanism, and we need to take good care of it. The average brain weighs three pounds and contains 12 billion cells which are each connected to ten thousand other brain cells. All together we have 120 billion brain connectors.

Dr. Gehad Dirk, who holds fifty patents on the IBM computer, said, "If we could invent a computer that would duplicate the capabilities of the human brain, it would take a structure the size of the Empire State Building just to house it." We need to be careful how we program our minds.

If we intend to follow Jesus in a corrupt and immoral generation, we need to remove all the X-rated videos from our brains. If we program garbage in, we will get garbage out. If we have any magazines, books, or videos that would be considered raunchy, it would be a good idea to bundle them up and haul them to the dump. We need to allow Jesus to clean house. If we have gotten in the habit of watching perverted movies or even suggestive TV, we need to stop. The Bible has enough cleansing power to scrub our brains clean.

For Discussion

1. When Peter was playing hide and seek in his dad's
   closet, was he wrong to look at the magazine the first
   time?
   Was it natural for him to desire another look?
   Was there anything wrong with the experience?

2. Why do we sometimes desire to look at private things?

3. List five negative effects pornography can have on us.

4. What does the author mean by *brainwashing?*
   What can scrub our brains clean?

5. In what way is the brain like a computer?

6. Why is it important to guard our thought lives?

7. Have you ever seen a pornographic picture?
   How did you react inside?

8. Do you have anything hiding in your room that could be
   morally damaging?
   Dirty pictures, records, tapes?
   Have you ever thought about hauling them to the dump?

eight

Kissing Contests

A mother of a teenage boy called me the other day. As I answered the phone, she was laughing hysterically, and she wanted to share her hilarious discovery with someone.

"While cleaning my son's room," she explained, "I was dusting his girlfriend's picture frame and noticed a note the girl wrote on the back of the picture. Listen to this:

> To My Dearest Michael,
>   I love you with all my heart—you are my one and only!
>   I love you more and more every day and I will love you forever—through all eternity. I am yours.
>   Sally
> P.S. If we ever break up, I want this picture back.

That story paints a very humorous picture of teenage infatuation. As young people, we have fully developed bodies and underdeveloped emotions. Our emotions can easily gain the upper hand and dominate everything we do.

Falling in Love

It is an incredible feeling when everything we have seen in Hollywood movies about the romantic chemistry of falling in love suddenly starts happening inside every organ of our bodies. It is almost a hormonal holocaust.

The guy or girl of our dreams walks into the room. Our eyes meet. We exchange smiles and then nervously look away. Our hearts thump and a huge thrill surges through our system. Our palms get damp. We swallow hard. We dare to take another look and find him or her looking right back at us. Our hearts beat faster. Everything in our bodies seems to be more alive than ever before. *This is the person of my dreams* we tell ourselves. Romantic love has taken root in our hearts just the way we have seen it happen on TV. The crazy thing is, we haven't even met each other.

Some girls love the feeling of love. That feeling can get them as high as any hallucinogenic drug. They love watching romantic love stories. They cut their teeth reading romantic novels. They never dreamed it would happen to them but now that it has, it gives new meaning to life. Romantic vibrations build some girls' self-esteem unlike any other relationship and they will bounce from boyfriend to boyfriend and from deeply serious relationship to deeply serious relationship in order to keep those vibrations flowing.

Some guys are just as bad. They bounce from hot romance to hot romance. They want every relationship to rival *Romeo and Juliet*.

To be blunt, I have found that many people who operate like this are insecure. They feel as though they must have control of the relationship. They want no loose ends. Open relationships are threatening. They insist on being possessive, infatuated, and ingrown.

When Romance Is Idolatry

Let me tell you a dramatic story which gives new meaning to the expression, "I love you with all my heart."

Last year near San Francisco, California, a fifteen-year-old boy named Felipe was strongly attracted to a girl at school named Donna. He learned that she suffered from an enlarged heart that made it very difficult for her to breathe. Doctors told Donna that she would need a heart transplant from another teenager which would be hard to find.

One day Felipe told his parents, "I'm going to die, and I'm going to give my heart to my girlfriend." It sounded dramatic—too dramatic. From all visible signs he was in perfect health.

On Saturday he woke up with a horrible headache. He couldn't walk. His family took him to the hospital and then he was flown by an air ambulance to another hospital where top neurosurgeons determined that a blood vessel had burst in his head. Felipe was brain dead. Only the respirator kept him alive. Within the next twenty-four hours his heart was removed and placed inside Donna's chest. The doctors called it "a perfect match." The body weight and heart tissue of Felipe seemed perfectly compatible with those of his girlfriend. The surgery was successful, and she survived. He literally loved her with all his heart.

This true story dramatically illustrates what sometimes happens when two people fall in love.

It is possible to get so infatuated with a boyfriend or girlfriend that we are unable to think of anything else. We dream of that person at night and see him or her every day. We are unhappy when we are not together. We lose our appetite for food. We can't sleep well. Our studies suffer. Our other friendships are neglected. We drop out of clubs or athletic teams. Basically, we eat, sleep, and breathe this other special person. Without knowing it, we have become warped, yet we are loving every minute of it.

It is one thing to give a heart in order to save a human life. This is even commendable. It is something else to give away all our emotional affections. That can be devastating.

Our emotions can be so explosive inside our bodies that at times we feel as though we are about to blow a hole through the sides of our intestines. When our emotions gain control over us, we are in trouble.

Smoochathon

When I learned there was such a thing as a kissing contest— a smoochathon—I thought it would be fun to compete. According to the 1978 edition of the *Guinness Book of World Records,* Candy Wessling and Klaus Wagher set the record at Springfield, Virginia, when they kissed for 124 hours and 51 minutes. A few years ago, two Japanese couples were trying to break the record for nonstop kissing in the front window of a downtown Tokyo department store. As I recall, they fell asleep before breaking the mark.

I have known several couples who appeared to be trying to set their own record. Couples at parties, at the park, or at the beach embrace for hours with lips interlocked. They seem to be chewing each other's gum. Their faces are touching but sometimes I often wonder if their minds aren't a million miles away.

On March 5, 1977, Jeff Henxler set a record kissing 3,225 girls in only eight hours at Regency Hall, Indiana—a rate of one per 8.93 seconds. I know some guys who seem to be aiming at setting a similar record of their own. They kiss every girl they get introduced to.

Somehow, we need to control the flow of gushy-gushy, lovey-dovey, kissy-face romantic mush which gets passed off as true love.

Kissing

Beware of someone who wants to kiss on the first date. I used to have the without-a-kiss-on-the-first-date-it-has-been-a-total-waste mentality. I have since grown up.

Anyone who tells you that kissing is not fun is a liar. In fact, for many healthy teenagers, it ranks at the top of their list of favorite things to do. When we reach our lips forward to touch the lips of someone from the opposite sex it can send more electricity through our bodies than if we stuck our finger in the wall socket. To enjoy the sensation of kissing does not mean we are strange. Quite the contrary, it shows that we are normal.

However, similar to sticking our fingers in the socket, kissing carries with it certain invisible dangers. Kissing literally gets our motors going. Prolonged kissing takes us up to very high speeds. And passionate kissing will send us over guardrails, down dead-end alleys, or even into a fatal head-on collision. Kissing presses the emotional pedal to the metal and there is no telling where we will end up.

If anyone wants to kiss on the first date, we need to be prepared to say no. Anyone who wants to kiss on the first date when he or she doesn't even know you probably expects to move into heavier physical involvement once he or she does get to know you. If your date wants to kiss you right away, what has he or she done already with other dates?

While a kiss is exciting and certainly appropriate as a relationship matures, it needs to be held in honor and not cheaply dispensed at the end of every date like a napkin or after-dinner mint.

"I Love You"

Beware of anyone who tells you he loves you on the first date. I was saying good night to a girl I had taken to the movies. It was the first time I had ever dated her. We had a great time that evening and it seemed to express the way I felt so I looked at her, smiled and said unashamedly, "I love you."

She looked back at me as if to say, "I'm sorry to hear you say that." If I did not have a great time with her that night I would have thought she was a goofball. But she explained, "My mother told me never to trust anyone who tells you *I love you* because he usually doesn't know what he means by it."

I hated to admit it, but she was right. Most people who say those three words have no idea what they are talking about. They might be trying to say all kinds of things.

- I want to impress you with how cool I am.
- I want to feel you out; what do you think of me?
- I care for you.
- I think you are special.
- I am wondering if I could kiss you.

Since the words *I love you* can often be motivated by pride, flattery, manipulation or just overstatement, they would be better avoided and even considered suspect.

My brother-in-law is impressive. He is a tall blond-haired basketball player from Grand Rapids. He never told any girl that he loved her until it was the girl he married. I applaud you, Tom Dykstra.

"Let's Pray Together"

Beware of anyone who wants to pray together on the first date. It amazes me that one of the most controversial things I tell teenage audiences around the country is that praying together is usually not a good idea until engagement. As we shall see, there are many reasons for this principle but the basic reason is because it takes the governor off the emotional gas pedal.

Too often the invitation *Let's pray together* is another way of saying:

- Let me show you how spiritual I am.
- Let me sprinkle a little holy water on the evening so that we won't feel guilty no matter what we do later on.
- I want to get inside your confidences, so let me get you to drop your defenses in prayer.
- I want this relationship to get intimate as fast as possible, so let's get intimate in prayer.

The three words *Let's pray together* often hide pride, manipulation, deceit, curiosity, and other ulterior motives, similar to the words *I love you.* Often couples start out holding hands in prayer. Then they graduate to praying with their arms around each other. Hey, if you can pray holding each other in your arms, just imagine what you can do when you stop praying. Prayer was never designed to be a smoke screen for unhealthy desires.

I know an effective Campus Life director who holds to the principle of not praying on dates ever since it almost blew up in his face. A sixteen-year-old girl came up to him crying after a meeting. They went outside under an old oak tree where she poured out her heart to him. Then they prayed. Innocent enough, right?

The next week the same girl came to him crying. "Can we go outside and talk again?" she asked. They talked and prayed, this time holding hands.

Next week she was not crying but she came up after the meeting. He took her by the hand, went out under the old oak tree, and they held each other in their arms and prayed.

The following week as they stood under the old oak tree kissing, my friend suddenly realized what was happening and he blew the whistle. "I would never have believed," he explained to me, "that praying together could get us so emotionally involved without even knowing it. I learned the hard way, but never again."

Emotional Control

Unless we control our emotions, our emotions will control us. There is nothing wrong with getting emotional. In fact, as we grow to love Jesus more and more, He deepens our capacity to experience a much wider range of emotions. Jesus Himself was a deeply emotional man. He sang and rejoiced with exhilarating joy, and on the other hand, He also cried when His friend died. He was moved with deep affection for people and at other times He raged with anger against injustice. But Jesus was always in control of His emotions and never allowed His emotions to control Him.

Most of us will never need to worry about lacking emotion. We have plenty to spare! However, we will all be in trouble if we allow our emotions to run our lives, to make our decisions, and to tell us what is right and wrong. Our generation has told us, "If it feels good, do it. Don't deny yourself any pleasure." Even pop singer Debbie Boone sang it in her golden hit song "You Light Up My Life," which asks how anything that feels right could be wrong.

If I swallow that lie and determine what is morally right and wrong according to what my emotions tell me, I will obey God only when I feel like it. What is right and wrong is no longer based on what God clearly says in the Bible, but rather it is determined by what I feel like inside. Once my emotions take control, Jesus loses control. At that point, I lose all self-control and I become a slave to my sinful desires. This is why it is essential for us to keep our emotions under control by maintaining some of the guidelines mentioned in this chapter.

Brothers and Sisters

If we keep our emotions under control and refuse to swallow the Hollywood lie about romantic love, we can discover a whole new level of relationship with the opposite sex—doing things together as brother and sister.

The Apostle Paul wrote his younger brother in Christ, Timothy, the following radical dating advice, "Treat older men like fathers, older women like mothers; younger men like brothers and younger women like sisters in all purity" (*see* 1 Timothy 5:1, 2).

Treating younger Christian women like sisters and younger Christian men like brothers is where all dating needs to start. If we get the hang of this concept it will be the most revolutionary thing since the world started turning. We can do things together as brother and sister without getting all emotionally supercharged, and it will help build mutual respect and dignity.

I have a sister with whom I have always had a very close relationship. Since she is six years older, we avoided much of the sibling conflicts and yet we were close enough in age that we spent many hours at home together. So when Paul says, "Treat younger women as sisters," I can relate.

There are a few obvious applications of characteristics of the brother-sister relationship worth emphasizing.

1. Just as I would never think of having sex with my sister, so I should never think of having sex with my sister in Christ. It should be repulsive even to consider.
2. Just as I would not expect my sister to make me look cool, I should never look to my sister in Christ as a status symbol—someone to date in order to look better in front of my friends.
3. Just as I would never think about marrying my sister, so I should not be sizing up all my sisters in Christ as whether or not they would make good marriage partners.
4. Just as I would stick up for my sister if she ever got in trouble, so I should seek to serve my sister in Christ, desiring God's best in her life.

When I was three years old my sister jumped out of a boat to save me from drowning. Similarly we should be willing to jump in and help each other as brothers and sisters in God's family.

Surely God intended dating for more than kissing contests and smoochathons. When our emotions are kept in check, meaningful, healthy relationships will be given room to develop naturally in due time.

Legal Age for Dating

Could you imagine the Congress of the United States passing a law that required people to be a certain age before they would be permitted to date? The U.S. Congress will never pass such a law, but some parents already have. I know parents who have told their teenagers they can't date until they are sixteen years old. Others have set the limit at fourteen. Some parents have set no such age limit.

As much as we hate to admit it, *early dating leads to early sex*. *USA Today* reported a study done of 2,400 teenagers which revealed an alarming trend: 91 percent of all the girls who start dating at twelve years of age will have sex by graduation, compared with 20 percent who start dating at sixteen years.

When our parents tell us we can't date until we are sixteen, it might sound as if they are telling us to hold our breath for four years. Actually, they probably have our best interest in mind. Whether we realize it or not, we will survive.

For Discussion

1. Describe the expression "head-over-heels in love."
    Have you ever experienced it?
    If so, tell your story.
    Do you think you will ever experience it in the future?
    How does it happen?

2. Describe Hollywood romance.
    List five characteristics of such a typical relationship.

3. When can a boy-girl relationship become *idolatry*?

4. Would you ever like to enter a kissing contest?
    Why or why not?

5. Why do many young people like to kiss on the first
    date?
    Do you think it's a good idea?
    Why or why not?

6. What different influences can motivate young couples
    to tell each other, "I love you"?

7. List three reasons the author warns against praying
    together while dating.
    Do you agree that it can be a problem?

8. Why is it important to keep our emotions under control?

9. List five ways a "brother-sister relationship" is different
    from the way most people date.

10. How can we determine when we are old enough to date?

11. If you were a parent of teenagers today, how would you
     prepare them to date?
     How old would you want your son or daughter to be
     before your teen started dating?
     What basis would you use to make that decision?

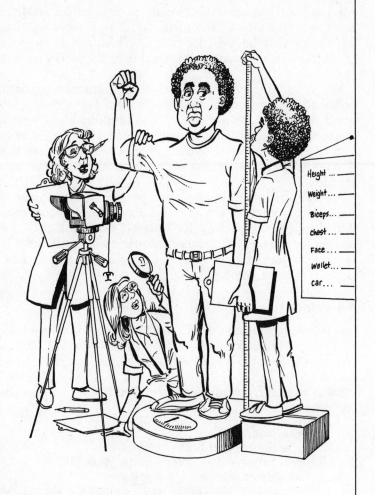

nine

The chart reads:
Height ...
Weight ...
Biceps ...
Chest ...
Face ...
Wallet ...
Car ...

Singleness Is Not
a Sickness

A friend of mine showed up at college his freshman year, took one look at the girls' dorm, and asked out loud, "Who's going to be the lucky lady? Which one of you eight hundred and fifty women will I select to be my wife? You lucky girl!"

Many of us are in a rut. Every time we meet a new guy or girl we silently ask the question, *Is this the one? Is this the one?* We spend a considerable amount of time thinking about who we are going to marry. Upperclassmen look over the incoming students to see who is eligible and who measures up to their standards. Underclassmen want to get in with a good crowd of friends.

I spend a couple of weeks every year on college campuses, and I always overhear conversation about marriage and courtship. It is easy, especially for college-aged women, to begin getting nervous at the prospect of graduating without a life partner. "Why did I bother going to college if I don't find a husband?" has become a cliché.

A Perfect 10

It is not uncommon for us even to develop our little list of qualities we are looking for—almost like a scorecard. Without even realizing it, we judge everyone we meet according to this list.

Some guys carry around an unwritten list of qualities they are looking for in a life partner.

1. Good looking
2. Trim figure, well-built
3. Good personality—laughs at my jokes
4. Shaves her legs and underarms
5. Nice family—gets along with her parents and brothers and sisters
6. Good Christian—straight, loves the Lord but not too stuffy about it

Girls also have their own list of qualities they are looking for in guys.

1. Nice looking—handsome
2. Polite; treats me nice; doesn't belch in public
3. Moral—doesn't just want to sit around and kiss all the time
4. Kind—thoughtful, generous, sends me cards

There is nothing wrong with having high standards for a life partner. In fact, even when just dating we would be insane not to have high standards for selecting the person with whom we might spend the rest of our lives. There is a real problem, however, when we use that standard to judge everyone we meet. If we start rejecting people because they are not perfect 10s, we are snobs.

Whenever we meet a new guy or girl we should not hold up our list and ask, *Is this the one?* because at the heart of the question we are saying, *What can you do for me?* This is essentially self-seeking. We don't want to get bogged down in the self-seeking strategies of spouse hunting. That can be a very nervous, meaningless exercise.

Often when we make a list of qualities we are looking for in a life partner, we include outward qualities and overlook the inward qualities. Everyone wants a marriage partner who has a pretty face, beautiful complexion, and perfect shape. But it is far more important to find a mate who is honest, kind, hardworking, conscientious and morally pure.

God's Scorecard

The Bible reminds us, "Man looks on the outward appearance but God looks on the heart" (*see* 1 Samuel 16:7). We need to understand there is more to choosing a life partner than just picking another pretty face. Marriage is a union of personalities. Marriage requires a blending of spirits and a deep admiration for the inner person, not just the outward appearance.

God gave me clearance to marry Sherry when I realized that although she is good looking and fun to be with, I actually loved her inner person more than her body.

I spent the summer after our freshman year of college on a

small island called Sanibel off the west coast of Florida in the Gulf of Mexico. She flew down to be with me for a last week of summer. Coming from Michigan, her skin was not used to the superhot direct sunrays. After one day at the beach she was covered with the ugliest sun rash I had ever seen. She broke out in black, molelike spots. She had one on her lip and a couple on her eyelids. If I do say so myself, she looked bad.

Fortunately, she was not in severe pain but she sure felt lousy about the way she looked. The amazing part of the story is that it was that rash that looked so gross that actually convinced me that I had the love needed to marry her. It showed me I was not attracted to her because of her good looks. I was attracted to her because of her inner qualities—her godliness, gentleness, and wisdom. I could imagine growing older together, and even if her hair fell out and her teeth rotted away, I would still love her because I loved the inner person.

This was important to me because it was important to God. I knew it was important to Him because He designed marriage and He intends it to be lifelong. If marriage is going to last that long it needs to be based on more than a girl's figure or a guy's hairline.

No Perfect People

It is ridiculous to keep a scorecard on everyone we meet, looking for the perfect person, because there is no such thing as a perfect person. If we ever get married thinking our spouse is perfect, we are in for a crushing disappointment. Someday we will wake up and smell his morning mouth or see her hair in curlers or find dental floss on the sink and suddenly realize we did not marry the perfect person.

Then what? What will we do when this perfect person we married gets the stomach flu and starts vomiting everywhere? What will we do if he or she is too sick to clean it up?

I'll tell you what many people do—they walk out. They file for divorce, not just because of a stomach flu but because their bubble burst. They suddenly and painfully realize their perfect mate has some tragic flaws.

We need to understand that carrying around a secret score-card to judge possible life partners will create an unrealistic level of expectation that will only lead to disappointment and unfulfillment.

Singles'-Bars Mentality

I don't know of many people who recommend going to a singles' bar to find a life partner. Someone might recommend going there to find a friend, a companion, or a one-night-stand, but not a marriage partner.

As severe as this might sound, some church young adult groups are not much different from a singles' bar. They are dominated by the same spirit. Divorcées and single people get together to socialize and flirt. Basically they attend the meetings to make a good impression in order to find a spouse. Such an atmosphere is not healthy and it is certainly not godly.

The Bible gives us a wonderful example of a young and very attractive widow who refused to give in to the singles'-bar mentality. The book containing her story is even named after her—Ruth. The entire book is only five pages long, but it contains some of the best courtship advice found anywhere. The Book of Ruth can be considered God's model for single people.

Here are some principles to consider for yourself:

1. When her first husband died, her thoughts were not for herself, but to fulfill her responsibilities to others (Ruth 1:1–15).
2. Choosing to leave her own country to move to a foreign country with her mother-in-law was a choice that meant she might forfeit finding a life partner, at least a spouse from her own race. She nevertheless chose to fulfill her responsibilities to serve her mother-in-law rather than seek after her own personal interests (1:6–22).
3. While Ruth was humbly serving her mother-in-law, godly character was being developed in her heart that made her very attractive to men of similar godly character (2:1–9).

4. When a handsome, wealthy man named Boaz approached her, Ruth was so overwhelmed that she bowed down to the ground and expressed genuine gratefulness. She obviously was not restless, anxious, or nervous about finding a spouse. She did not come on strong. She did not flirt. She was humble, modest, and taken by surprise (2:10–21).

5. When Ruth began taking an interest in this man, she still asked permission from her mother-in-law before she allowed the relationship to develop (2:22–3:8).

6. Ruth was committed to marry only God's choice for her. According to Hebrew custom, a widow was to marry the next closest male who was known as the kinsman redeemer. Even though she might have found someone more handsome, younger, or wealthier, she would submit to the proper limitation of her moral law. This hard choice showed her inner beauty to Boaz more than anything. He referred to her as "a woman of noble character" (3:11). He loved her inner person of the heart as well as her outer person (3:9–18).

7. The real evidence that Ruth's courtship was exemplary is that she was the great grandmother of King David and the great, great, great . . . grandmother of Jesus (ch. 4). She is an excellent model of a godly woman, a widow, a daughter-in-law, a wife, and a mother.

The Gift of Singleness

Jesus was never married, and He was normal. Paul was not married, and he was normal. John the Baptist was single, and he was normal. History is full of normal men and women who were never married. We need to understand that *one is a whole number*.

Beyond this, God actually calls some people to remain single for life. He gives them the sacred gift of singleness on behalf of the Kingdom (1 Corinthians 7:7, 8; Matthew 19:12). Just as Jesus wonderfully shows Himself as a father to the orphan and husband to the widow, so He will satisfy the deep needs of the single person. He promises to do that. This is a benefit God wants all single people to receive from Him (1 Corinthians 7:17).

When God calls some of us to be married, we will exchange the one gift of singleness for the gift of marriage. We are never without a gift and calling of grace to keep us content in the state we are in.

I'm Yours

There is in the heart of every person a deep desire to say to another person, "Take me, I'm yours!" Those who are called to singleness need to say this to Jesus.

Jesus never said, "Seek ye first a life partner." He said, "Seek ye first the Kingdom of God." (*See* Mathew 6:33.) Those who are given the gift of singleness are given greater freedom to invest time, money, and energy into the needs of the Kingdom (1 Corinthians 7:32–35).

I received an exciting letter from my friend Mike yesterday. Let me share it with you.

Dear Fred,
  Can you remember praying with me last summer in Colorado about my need for a wife? You told me to give my desires to Jesus; basically, to say to Him, *I'm Yours. I give my heart to You and I receive the gift of singleness from You.* Well, God took my anxieties away and I was very content serving the Lord as a single person and youth minister here in the church. But it looks like God had a better idea.
  In November I started dating Beth. She recently graduated from Bible college and was hoping to pursue a career in missions. We were engaged in March and are looking toward a July wedding. God has made it very clear to us that we can serve Him better together and that He has called us to commit ourselves to one another in marriage.
  I felt like you played a part in getting me ready for marriage when we prayed together that night, so I wanted to share my joy with you. Thanks.
                                          Your friend,
                                          Mike

Mike is a wonderful example of a 1980s pacesetter who is experiencing the excellence of doing things God's way. He learned firsthand the wonderful joy of Proverbs 19:14: "Houses and wealth are inherited from parents, but a prudent wife is from the Lord."

We don't need to waste our time and energy like fools, frantically hunting spouses. God wants us to be content as single people, to be grateful for the gift of singleness, to have a mind and heart to serve Him, and to treat the opposite sex like brothers and sisters. If, to our surprise, God chooses to give us the gift of marriage, I'm sure we won't object.

For Discussion

1. Have you ever felt pressured to get married?
    How did it feel?

2. List four good reasons to get married.

3. List four lousy reasons for getting married.

4. List five qualities you look for in a spouse, in order of
    importance.

5. Is it healthy to use these qualities to evaluate people?
    What are some potential dangers?

6. How can a church youth group resemble a singles' bar?

7. What qualities did you admire in the Bible lady Ruth?

8. What is meant by "the gift of singleness"?

9. What are some dangers of chasing after a marriage
    partner?

ten

A Look Over
the Threshold

We have all looked down from the top of a tall building, or perhaps over a cliff down into the Grand Canyon. We have felt the butterflies and the sick feeling in the pit of our stomachs as we say to ourselves, *What would happen if I ever fell from up here?*

While standing with your toes dangling over the edge, have you ever had someone you thought was your friend sneak up behind you and give you a sudden bump? You gasp! You experience an instant adrenaline surge. Your heart thumps. Your life passes before you. Every organ in your body prepares for a free-fall. Then you realize your friend has a firm grip on your belt and bumped you as a joke. Ha! Ha! Ha! Instead of laughing, you feel like punching his lights out!

Thinking about marriage should be no less awesome. Every time we think about saying, "I do," we should feel just as overwhelmed and horrified as when we look over the edge from a great height. Marriage is overwhelming. To consider committing ourselves to live with one person for the rest of our life should be awesome enough to take the breath away from any rational person.

Looking into marriage is as fascinating as following Jacques Cousteau on an underwater guided tour of a coral reef. We will discover things we have never seen before—things we never thought existed. In many ways it is a whole new world that is beyond description.

"Dad, I'm Scared"

After dating Sherry for seven months, we were sitting on a park bench feeding pigeons. All of a sudden the unthinkable crawled across my brain—*Will you marry me?* I panicked. I gulped. My eyes bugged out, and my mouth hung open. I stared at her, but I couldn't say anything. My hands sweated. I had goose bumps the size of marbles all over my body. She asked me what was wrong, and I couldn't say a word. I felt trapped, and I needed breathing room.

I walked her to her dormitory and then ran to the closest pay phone to call my dad. I needed help fast. I had never been so scared in my life.

"Dad, are you alone? I've got to talk with you about something really important."

After I assured him I wasn't in jail or the hospital, I told him why I felt such urgency. "Dad, I have never felt this way before. I am really scared. You know I have been dating this girl Sherry. Well, lately when we're together, things are happening inside my body that I have never felt before. Tonight we were just sitting there talking and I got this sick feeling. I don't know if you ever felt like this before or not but the four words just kept crawling across my mind. It's really hard to even say these words out loud." I hemmed and hawed and stuttered and stammered for forty-five minutes over long distance before I could get it out. "Dad, what do you do when everything inside you is telling you there is no other option than to get married? There is nothing sexual, but emotionally I just can't handle it. I don't know if you have ever been through something like this, but what do I do?"

"Fred," my father responded matter-of-factly, "what's your problem? Do you think you are the first person to ever fall in love?" I realized it was a little silly to think that my dad had never felt deep love for anyone. After all, he was married to my mother! But I must admit, even though I felt a little foolish, I was overwhelmingly relieved to find out that he could identify with me and that I was normal.

He reminded me, "Fred, if you didn't feel overwhelmed at the possibility of marriage, you would have something wrong with you. Marriage is a big deal. You only make that decision once in your life and you need to make it carefully."

As I recall, we talked for another forty-five minutes about how to tell when it is the right person. When we finished talking, I didn't have all the answers I felt I needed but at least I knew I was asking the right questions, and I sure was glad I'd called collect.

Flash in the Pan

Too many people in our generation still look at marriage as a trial balloon—the old try-it-you'll-like-it routine.

In our day of fast foods, instant coffee, and Minute Rice, it is hard to believe that anything good is worth waiting for. In a day of disposable bottles, disposable razors, and disposable diapers, it is hard to believe in anything other than disposable girlfriends, disposable fiancés, and disposable spouses. Marriage almost falls in the easy-come-easy-go, flash-in-the-pan category.

We are bombarded with soap operas and romantic Hollywood productions that preach to us about fast cars, fast fun, and fast marriages. Even the true-to-life love stories of rock stars and movie stars seem to paint a wonderful picture of love at first sight and marriages made in heaven. They seem to suggest that any moral laws or forethought or calculations would cramp our style. As the saying goes, "All is fair in love and war."

A nineteen-year-old Ohio State student said, "Sex should be spontaneous and exciting, not premeditated. All that planning really puts a chill on the thrill." It is no wonder his girlfriend got pregnant last year and was forced to face the responsibilities of his irresponsibility.

Basically, our generation suffers from a bad case of nearsightedness. Too many red-hot lovers are moving at such a feverish pace they can't see straight. They can see things happening now, but feel threatened and insecure when asked to think about tomorrow. However, somewhere deep down inside we know there is more to courtship than a flash-in-the-pan, hot-sizzle romance.

At times we look at marriage with the same excitement and commitment as getting a new pair of shoes. When we buy them and wear them out of the store, they make us feel really great about ourselves. We think we are floating six inches off the ground. But later when they get soiled or out of style, we know we can get a new pair. If they are not comfortable or if they don't match what we're wearing, we can always give them to the Salvation Army. A new pair of shoes brings high excitement but very superficial commitment.

Commitment is what marriage is all about. If we look at our marriage partner as someone simply to make us feel good about ourselves for a while, we are in for a major disappointment. We might get all caught up in the mushy-gushy feeling of love but such feelings won't last any longer than a pair of new shoes.

Commitment

We are seeing a surprising reaction to widespread divorce. Because most families have been touched by separation, the children of broken homes are rediscovering the need of solid commitment in marriage. Those who have felt the sting of their parents' separation have learned firsthand that marriage is nothing to mess around with. They never want to put their children through the agony they have felt. Many long for stability and permanence, and therefore are shifting the trend back to holding marriage in honor.

In a day when 1.2 million children every year join the ranks of "divorced kids," the U.S. Census Bureau says 12.8 million kids live with a single parent and an additional 7.8 million kids live with step-families, and when public school psychologists say that the cause of most mental health problems for kids is the emotional turmoil of living through a divorce, there is a chance that our generation which has weathered the worst marital storm in history, will break the cycle of divorce and no longer look at the marriage covenant as a revolving door.

Couples are choosing one of two new trends in regard to the marriage covenant: (1) avoiding getting married altogether and just living together; or (2) joining in marriage only after they are confident enough to permanently commit themselves.

As a minister, I invest more counseling time talking with soon-to-be-married couples than with any other group. In a day when almost one out of two marriages ends in divorce or separation, I have a responsibility to offer as much preventative medicine as possible. I will not perform a wedding ceremony unless the couple is able to meet with me for four one-hour sessions. This is one of the most fun and exciting aspects of my weekly routine. I am the minister of a young congregation so I perform a number of weddings each year. This means I do my share of premarital counseling.

At our first meeting, I ask both the prospective bride and groom to fill out a confidential survey sheet so that I can get to know them rather quickly (*see* Appendix II, "Premarital Survey"). I ask them to define the words *love* and *marriage,* and I ask them, "Why do you think *now* is the right time to get married?"

Before any couple repeats their wedding vows they need to be sure they are willing to remain faithful through thick and thin. If they are not ready to keep the commitment, they ought not make it.

As we have seen, emotions need to be kept under control so they do not control us. When it comes to marriage, emotions will never hold us together. This is why commitment is so important. Commitment is what marriage is made out of because commitment is what love is made out of.

Songwriter Don Francisco creatively expresses the need for couples to stand behind their marriage commitment even when they don't feel like it.

Love Is Not a Feeling

So you say you can't take it, the price is too high
The feelings have gone,
*   It seems the river's run dry*
You never imagined it could turn out so rough
You give and give and give and still
*   It's never enough*
Your emotions have vanished,
*   that once held a thrill*
You wonder if love could be alive in you still
But that ring on your finger
*   was put there to stay*
You'll never forget the words
*   you promised that day*
Jesus didn't die for you because it was fun
He hung there for love because
*   it had to be done*
And in spite of the anguish,
*   His word was fulfilled*

> 'Cause love is not a feeling, it's an act of your will
> Love is not a feeling, it's an act of your will
> Now I wouldn't try to tell you
>   that it's easy to stand
> When Satan's throwing everything
>   that's at his command
> But Jesus is faithful, His promise is true
> And the things that He asks,
>   He gives the power to do.

God's Invention

God is the mastermind who invented marriage. He is the architect and engineer who first drew up the master plan and put the pieces together. And He is the Supreme Counselor who gives excellent advice to keep marriages running smoothly.

Very briefly let me set forth seven of God's guidelines for marriage.

1. Marriage is a lifelong commitment between one man and one woman.

For this reason a man shall leave his father and mother and shall cleave to his wife and the two shall become one flesh.

See Genesis 2:24

2. Divorce is not to be considered an option.

"I hate divorce," says the Lord. . . .

Malachi 2:16

He answered, "Anyone who divorces his wife and marries another woman commits adultery against her. And if she divorces her husband and marries another man, she commits adultery."

Mark 10:11, 12

3. A man and woman are not married until they make their wedding vows publicly in the sight of God and man.

What ... God has joined together, let not man put asunder.

Mark 10:9 RSV

... She is your ... wife by covenant.

Malachi 2:14 RSV

4. Up until the public wedding covenant, couples are to exercise self-control and abstain from sexual activity.

Marriage should be honored by all, and the marriage bed kept pure, for God will judge the adulterer and all the sexually immoral.

Hebrews 13:4

For this is the will of God, your sanctification; that you abstain from unchastity; that each one of you know how to take a wife for himself in holiness and honor, not in the passion of lust like heathen who do not know God.

1 Thessalonians 4:3–5 RSV

5. Once we are married, any sexual activity outside of marriage is plainly off limits. We shouldn't even think about it.

"You have heard that it was said, 'Do not commit adultery.' But I tell you that anyone who looks at a woman lustfully has already committed adultery with her in his heart."

Matthew 5:27, 28

6. Within marriage sexual activity is a blast. It is intended for pleasure as well as producing babies.

May your fountain be blessed, and may you rejoice in the wife of your youth. A loving doe, a graceful deer—may her breasts satisfy you always, may you ever be captivated by her love.

Proverbs 5:18, 19

The husband should fulfill his marital duty to his wife,
and likewise the wife to her husband. The wife's body
does not belong to her alone but also to her husband. In
the same way, the husband's body does not belong to him
alone but also to his wife.

1 Corinthians 7:3, 4

7. Marriage partners are to serve each other in love.
Wives are to submit to their husbands' loving leadership and be supportive of their best interests. Husbands are to sacrificially love their wives by even
laying down their lives if necessary.

Submit to one another out of reverence for Christ. Wives,
submit to your husbands as to the Lord.

Ephesians 5:21, 22

Wives, in the same way be submissive to your husbands
so that, if any of them do not believe the word, they may
be won over without words by the behavior of their
wives. . . . Husbands, in the same way be considerate as
you live with your wives, and treat them with respect as
the weaker partner and as heirs with you of the gracious
gift of life, so that nothing will hinder your prayers.

1 Peter 3:1, 7

When marriage is practiced according to God's design there
is no more enjoyable relationship this side of heaven. Such a
marriage is fun, fulfilling, exciting, challenging, and invigo-
rating. Speaking as a happily married man, the physical
expression of love is awesome. It is exhilarating, and it is
worth waiting for.

Despite popular opinion, however, good marriages don't just
happen, they require hard work. While God certainly plays a
part in the selection and appointment of marriage partners,
successful marriages don't just drop out of the sky. It is
ridiculous to think that good athletes don't practice or that
good gardens don't require weeding. Good hairstyles still
require washing, blow drying, and combing. Good cars still
require tune-ups and maintenance. And good marriages also
require work.

Until we are ready to make the commitment and put forth the effort, we are not ready to say, "I do."

Heads Up!

You might be wondering, *After having told us not to waste thought and energy searching for the right marriage partner, why does he now tell us to be so careful about whom we marry?*

There are two extremes we need to avoid when anticipating marriage. On the one hand, some of us constantly think about it. We size up everyone as a possible life partner by asking, *Is this the one?* The other extreme is to stick our heads in the sand and hide from any thought of marriage.

When the topic of marriage comes up, some of us respond, "Hey, don't talk to me about that! That's years away. I don't want to think about that until I'm older." This response may be typical but it is also tragic. It is ignorant to deny the connection between our present dating habits and our possible future marriage. However, we need to date each other today knowing that we will someday probably marry someone else.

Once we get our heads out of the sand, it is healthy to take a long look over the edge into the awesomeness of marriage. But once we look over the edge it would be odd to become so obsessed with the view that we spend all our time just standing there looking. We never want to forget the awesomeness of the sight, but we need to get on with the rest of life.

For Discussion

1. Why does the author compare marriage to looking over the edge of the Grand Canyon?

2. How did he feel when he first called his dad to ask advice about marriage?

3. A nineteen-year-old said, "Sex should be spontaneous. . . . All that planning really puts a chill on the thrill." Do you agree or disagree?

4. What is marriage based on?
   What holds it together?

5. List three ways we can avoid divorce.

6. How does God's view of marriage differ from the way many people see it today?

eleven

Sex Ed 101

If when reading the table of contents, your curiosity was aroused by this chapter title and you decided to start reading here first . . . *I gotcha!* I guarantee you now that the things you will read in this chapter will be things you never heard in any sex-ed class in school.

Some parents have problems telling their children the truth about sex and how babies are born. I recently heard about a thirteen-year-old boy who asked his mother where she came from. She told him an elaborate story about a beautiful bird with white feathers. The boy then went into the next room and privately asked his grandmother where she came from. She told him a variation of the bird story. The boy then ran next door and said to his buddy, "Good grief! There hasn't been a normal birth in our family for three generations."

Some parents have waited so long to talk with their children about sex, when they finally get around to it, the young person has already learned the facts through the grapevine.

Our parents don't need to be embarrassed as they talk with us about our private body parts and reproduction. Male and female sex organs are not dirty; they are holy. This is why we should not joke in the locker room about sex or look at pornographic pictures. It is not that sex is dirty; sex is holy, and holy things must not be treated as commonplace or ordinary. Sex is so extraordinary and special that it needs to be treated with modesty and honor.

Professor Flutesnoot

Many public schools think they teach sex ed but they don't. Trying to teach sex education without teaching moral values is like trying to teach riflery without teaching the way to point the gun. It is like trying to teach driver's ed without teaching on which side of the road we drive. Rifles and handguns can be dangerous weapons if they are mishandled. Automobiles can likewise be fatal if they are not used cautiouslv. Even more so, sex can blow up in our faces and take innocent lives if it is not channeled properly. It must be kept within certain moral guidelines.

Professor Flutesnoot in biology class or Mrs. McGuilicutty in P.E. may teach us how to load the gun but they do not point us to the rifle range. In public school we will see vivid diagrams. We will be shown parts of the human anatomy both on the inside and outside, some of which we never before knew even existed. We will learn about how babies are made and we might even watch a graphically bloody film of an actual birth. We will probably be taught about contraception, pills, condoms, foam, and diaphragms. We will be taught about the various forms of venereal disease and shown full-color slides of each one's advanced symptoms (gross!). But there is one key area conspicuously missing—moral values. Teachers of sex education are embarrassingly silent about any guidelines of right and wrong. Like driving instructors who teach us how to start the car, buckle our seatbelts, and accelerate, they hand us the keys and send us out without telling us anything about the brakes. Sex education without brakes is a guaranteed disaster. It is no wonder so many teenagers are ending up in the scrap heap.

Steven Muller, president of Johns Hopkins University, said, "The failure to rally around a set of values means that universities are turning out potentially highly skilled barbarians."

Even the U.S. Surgeon General, Dr. C. Everett Koop said, "I don't think sex education should be taught value-free. I think if you try to teach sex education value-free, what you are teaching is sexual techniques."

We want to look at four essential words which are not taught in the study of sex in public school: *virginity, fidelity, innocence,* and *modesty*.

Virginity

When I was in the sixth grade, I can remember walking on the beach and reading a T-shirt which said, "Virginity is a disease—help stamp it out." I turned to my friend and asked a very logical question, "What is *virginity?*" As I recall, he did not know either.

Virginity is a commitment. Virginity says, "I know that my sexuality is too sacred—too special—to waste. I am committed to saving it for my marriage partner, and I will keep saving it until I make the marriage commitment. My body belongs to Jesus, and I will not compromise. Anything less than that is selling myself short."

Our generation has sold themselves short. They have lost the value of virginity and consequently they are paying the price. Many of those who called virginity a disease a few years ago are now suffering from another disease. The joke is on them but no one is laughing. Venereal disease is epidemic.

Perhaps your sex-ed teacher used the word *virginity*, but it most likely was not held in honor. They don't give varsity letters in virginity. There is no "Virgin of the Year" award. Virgins will not necessarily even get an A in sex-ed class. In fact, we might get called names like "Holy Joe," "Prude," "Queen Victoria" or even "Goody-Goody Two Shoes." Rather than getting honor, we might receive dishonor.

There was a time not very long ago, prior to the sexual revolution of the sixties, when those guilty of immorality were marked with an imaginary scarlet letter *A* for adultery. The times have changed and today virgins are the ones marked— with the imaginary scarlet letter *V*. Our generation might mock virginity. God applauds it. He finds great value in virginity. If you are a virgin, you should square your shoulders, lift your face, and wear the letter *V* proudly! You are not sick. You are healthy. And you can help start a second sexual revolution. You can overthrow the popular trends and rediscover God's standards.

Obviously you don't need to advertise your virginity. If you run for class president you don't need to put it on your résumé. If you graduate valedictorian, you don't need to put it in your graduation speech. The very nature of virginity is modest and discreet and would prefer keeping the secret private.

Fidelity

At a youth group meeting I used the word *fidelity* and one kid spoke up, "I thought you were going to talk on sex, not stereo equipment." I chuckled to myself, but then I realized most of us hear the word used only as "high fidelity."

Fidelity means "a faithful devotion to fulfill a duty; to accurately copy the original." A good stereo system has high fidelity which means it is able to sound just like the original without distortion; it is a clear, clean sound. A good value system also has high fidelity; it faithfully follows God's original design without distortion.

If we listen to the music coming from most dating relationships around us, it will sound nothing like what God originally intended. Like a lousy stereo system, dating without fidelity is nothing but noisy static. God intends for us to make music together and in order for that to happen, we must submit to God's moral standards.

Fidelity says, "I will only be a one-woman man or a one-man woman. I will not only maintain virginity prior to marriage, if God calls me into marriage, I will continue to maintain fidelity." Fidelity says to God, "Because my sex organs are so holy and special, I commit them to You. I will not abuse them but rather I will faithfully exercise self-control." Fidelity says to our dates, "I will treat you with respect and I expect you to do the same with me." If married, fidelity says, "Our marriage is exclusive. I will look nowhere else to have my marital needs met, and I commit myself to meet your needs first."

Innocence

There is a strong curiosity built into every one of us to learn firsthand about private things. When Peter was playing hide and seek in his dad's closet and the *Playboy* magazine fell off the shelf, he took a second look even though something inside said no. His conscience and his curiosity were in conflict, and his curiosity won. Usually sometime during childhood we see a picture or walk in on someone while they are dressing and our curiosity about sex becomes aroused. We want to see more. The curiosity itself is normal. How we respond to the curiosity can be harmful.

Let me give you a tip which could save you a few scrapes and scars: *Trying to satisfy our sexual curiosity by giving in to it is like trying to put out a fire with gasoline.*

Some adults have never learned this lesson. They look at more and more magazines, attend more and more X-rated movies and hire more and more prostitutes. When erotic pleasures stop giving the thrill, they turn to even worse perversions of men having sex with men, and women with women, humans with animals, or even with dead corpses. As sick as such a life-style sounds, it happens because people have not learned that sexual curiosity arouses an appetite that cannot be properly satisfied. One look desires another look. Buying one dirty magazine leads to buying another. Taking clothes off one person produces the desire to take clothes off another person.

Our generation says, "You don't know what you're talking about until you've tried it. You need to experience it firsthand. Try it, you might like it." Our generation mocks innocence and makes it synonymous with ignorance.

There are many things that would be stupid to experience firsthand. It would be stupid to stick a knife into an electrical outlet. It would be stupid to drink poison. It would be stupid to leap from a cliff thinking, *I might be able to fly.* It would also be just as stupid to experiment with something God has already labeled POISON! OFF LIMITS! DANGER! KEEP OUT!

The Bible says, ". . . I want you to be wise about what is good, and innocent about what is evil" (Romans 16:19) or as it says in another translation, "I want to see you experts in good, and not even beginners in evil" (PHILLIPS).

Innocence is the quality of being free from the knowledge of evil by experience. Innocence is freedom. It's freedom from guilt and lust and bondage to bad habits. Innocence is a freedom God wants every one of us to enjoy.

Innocence is not ignorance. We can know what is evil and harmful without experiencing it firsthand. Just as it would be stupid to sample a bottle labeled POISON, so we don't need to mess around with areas God has ruled out of bounds.

"Safe sex" is the new expression. Safe sex has been around for six thousand years, ever since God told man to limit sex to marriage. Our generation talks about birth control, God talks about self-control.

Modesty

Some girls think they need to wear string bikinis or blouses without bras in order to get guys to pay attention. Most girls have seen enough billboards and advertisements to realize that guys are attracted by the sight of skin. However, is skin what you want guys to notice about you? If so, what kind of guy are you after?

I noticed a pattern when I was in high school: Girls who dressed immodestly were often insecure and attempting to compensate for not feeling good about themselves. On the other hand, I noticed another pattern: Guys who liked immodestly dressed girls were usually after the wrong things.

Modesty is a quality I always looked for in a girl. In fact, my mother told me never to date a girl who didn't blush.

Modesty is the mark of inner beauty that outshines the outward physical beauty. It is the quiet confidence that knows it is good but that doesn't need to strut around or boastfully try to prove it to others.

Modesty doesn't need piles of makeup and mascara. Modesty is beautiful all by itself. Modesty doesn't need to make a good impression on others in order to feel good about itself. It knows it's good!

These four words—*virginity, fidelity, innocence,* and *modesty*—are powerful. Revolutionary. They give purpose, meaning, and direction to sex education. They are beauty marks which can characterize each of our lives.

For Discussion

1. Why are parents sometimes embarrassed to talk with us about sex?

2. If your parents have talked with you about sex, what grade would you give them on their presentation? A, B, C, D, F?
   How did you feel while they were talking?

3. Statistically, 25 percent of teenagers give their parents honest answers about sex questions.
   Do you?
   Why or why not?

4. If you had a sex-ed class at school, did they teach you values?
   What did they teach?

5. What is the value of virginity?

6. In your own words, define *fidelity*.

7. How is *innocence* different from *ignorance*?

8. From God's perspective, what is *"safe sex"*?

9. Define *modesty*.

twelve

My Body

Members of the opposite sex make us self-conscious about our physical appearance. It doesn't take us long to realize that the beautiful people seem to have more fun and more dates. Our friends with the pretty faces seem to be the most popular and those with the well-developed bodies seem to have the most self-confidence. Every year it seems that the homecoming queen is escorted to the prom by either the starting quarterback or the student council president. We can stand for hours in front of the mirror, trying to make the best of what we have, but we have all watched enough beauty pageants to realize we will never win a prize. We will never be a cover girl or Hollywood star. We might have a heart full of gold but we know we will never be popular if we have a face like a warthog.

The competition can get so intense in the locker room and hallways across this country, we can easily feel inferior. One high school in Minnesota sponsored a "Nerd Day" during which all students were encouraged to dress up and comb their hair like nerds. The day before the big event a young man named Clyde was teased unmercifully. His classmates told him he wouldn't need to change a thing. "Just come as you are. You'll win first place!" Ha! Ha! Ha! Everyone laughed . . . everyone but Clyde. He felt he had taken enough abuse. He went home hurting bad inside. Later that evening his parents found him dead. He hanged himself.

Face it, when we feel outclassed it hurts. We get angry when we know we are not as pretty or smart or talented as someone else.

Our bodies can cause us fits but I have good news: *God cares*. When we are not impressed with what we look like and when no one else seems to be very impressed either, He is. There are at least five good reasons why our bodies are very important to God.

Reason #1: He Designed My Body

I went to Children's Variety Hospital in Miami to visit one of the kids in our congregation. As I approached the front door, being wheeled out was a girl with no legs. I walked onto an elevator to see a baby in a metal cage with tubes sticking from several places on his body. As I got off the elevator, a kid with leg braces was hobbling down the hallway. I looked in the first room to see a badly deformed burn victim. The second room contained a Down's syndrome child. Inside I hurt. There was not an ounce of humor or a ray of sunshine in my heart. I stopped in the hall, hung my head, and thought for a moment about all the teenagers who feel inferior, deformed, unskilled, and socially handicapped. *What can parents tell these children that will help them feel loved and special and respectable? How can the nurses handle it, let alone build the self-esteem of these children?*

I lifted my head and looked in the nurses' station to see a plaque that seemed to put everything back in perspective. The lettering was written in child's print: I'M SOMEBODY, CAUSE GOD DON'T MAKE NO JUNK. I thought to myself, *That's it! That's the message we need to communicate to our generation.*

We need to understand that we are each very special. We need to hear God say, "I made you and I don't make any nerds." Every one of us is eligible to wear a label that says CUSTOM-MADE, HANDCRAFTED, ORIGINAL, ONE OF A KIND, MADE BY THE MASTER CRAFTSMAN.

The Bible says, "For you created my inmost being; you knit me together in my mother's womb. My frame was not hidden from you when I was made in the secret place. When I was woven together in the depths of the earth, your eyes saw my unformed body. All the days ordained for me were written in your book before one of them came to be" (Psalms 139:13, 15, 16).

[For more fun reading on the subject of self-acceptance and self-esteem read *Flops,* by Fred Hartley, published by Revell.]

Reason #2: He Purchased My Body

Sometimes we forget that God's forgiveness did not come cheap. In order for God to be able to say to us, "I forgive you," it cost Him the life of His only Son Jesus. We've heard those

words before but let me tell you a story that will help you feel
what they mean.

A drawbridge operator raised and lowered the railroad track
in order to allow riverboats to pass safely underneath. The
man was a faithful worker, and one day his son visited him to
learn what his father did every day. Like most boys, he was
quite curious. He climbed down through a trapdoor that was
left open so his father could keep an eye on the machinery.

Suddenly the boy lost his footing and slipped. He tumbled
into the gear mechanism and caught his ankle. The boy
screamed and tried to loosen his foot. His dad grabbed the boy's
arm and pulled desperately, but they were both unsuccessful.
Then a train sounded its whistle in the distance. Full of
passengers, the train was approaching and the fast-moving
locomotive could not possibly stop. The man needed to lower
the bridge.

What do I do? the man cried. *If I lower the bridge, I will crush
my son in the gears. But if I do not lower the bridge, everyone on
the train will crash.* Frantically he tried one last time to yank
his son to safety. He could not. He grabbed the lever in his
hands, took one last look at his son, and then with tears
streaming down his cheeks, he pulled hard. The large gears
began moving. He couldn't bear to watch his son's death. The
bridge clamped in place just in time to save the train. The man
hung his head and wept bitterly. He chose to save the lives of
many but it cost him the life of his son.

You and I needed safe passage from death to life but there
was no bridge. The only way God could possibly save us was to
sacrifice His only Son in the process. It hurt God the Father.
His Son had to die the violent death of crucifixion. We receive
forgiveness and eternal life for free, but it cost Jesus everything.

When the train passed overhead some passengers slept,
others were laughing or eating. No one realized the price the
bridge operator paid for their safety. So too, many of us still
show little regard and appreciation for what Jesus went
through in order for Him to be able to say, "I forgive you."
Forgiveness didn't come cheap, and we must not treat it
lightly.

Because of the price Jesus paid for us, we have been purchased. We no longer belong to ourselves, we now belong to Jesus.

The Bloody Mother

Bill is a student at a graduate school in California. Listen to him as he tells his story about the day he thought he might have killed his mother.

"When I was a young boy I fell in love with golf, and my parents gave me a club and a harmless whiffle-type golf ball which I could hit around the backyard. I loved to swing the club and feel it hit the ball—even though it would not go very far because of its lightness and all the holes in it. One day, thinking my parents weren't home, I had the overwhelming temptation to feel the click of a real ball against the club head. I teed it up and gave it a hard whack. Unfortunately the ball was not hit properly and it hooked sharply from its intended flight and the ball went directly for one of the windows of our house and right through the window with a terrifying crash. But the crash was immediately followed by a piercing scream. Oh, no! I ran for the house, burst into the living room, and there, standing in front of the window was my mother, bleeding. I gasped. What had I done? I cried out, 'Mother, I could have killed you!' She hugged me and said, 'I'm okay. It's all right. I'm going to be all right.' "

Then Bill said, "There in that moment—when I saw my mother bleeding—I knew there were some things I could never do again in the backyard. I could never so much as carry a golf club across the lawn of our backyard. The sight of her standing there with blood flowing down—that I had caused—changed my behavior forever."

When we see Jesus bleeding on the cross and we realize He hung there as a result of our disobedience, there will be certain things we will never be able to do again. Since Jesus died for *my* sins, it is sometimes helpful for us to picture ourselves actually punishing Jesus.

I ripped off His shirt and crushed a crown of thorns on His forehead. *I* took the leather whip and cracked it thirty-nine times across His bare back. *I* spit in His open wounds. *I* mocked Him and slapped Him and pulled whiskers from His face. *I* threw Him on the wooden beam, stretched out His arms, and drove spikes through His wrists and ankles. *I* lifted up His body on that cross and then gambled for His clothes and offered Him a vinegar cocktail. *I* plunged the spear in His side. Then *I* saw Him look at me through eyes of compassion and speak the words, "Father, forgive *this one*."

Today when I picture Jesus bleeding and when I realize that my sin and disobedience caused His blood to flow, sin very quickly loses its attraction. Disobedience becomes disgusting. I want nothing more than to change my behavior. I gladly recognize His ownership over me.

Reason #3: He Lives in My Body

One of the most exciting benefits of being a Christian is that I know that Jesus lives inside my body. He said, ". . . I am with you always . . ." (Matthew 28:20 RSV) and again, "I will never fail you nor forsake you" (Hebrews 13:5 RSV).

When I was a kid traveling with my parents in the Midwest, we saw the little house in which Abraham Lincoln lived. It was nothing spectacular in itself. In fact, it looked as though it was ready to fall apart, but the only reason it was special was because of the person who lived there.

We might not feel all that special but we are special because Jesus lives inside us. My body is His home. This is why the Bible says, ". . . The body is not meant for sexual immorality, but for the Lord, and the Lord for the body . . . Flee from sexual immorality . . . Do you not know that your body is a temple of the Holy Spirit, who is in you, whom you have received from God? You are not your own; you were bought at a price. Therefore honor God with your body" (1 Corinthians 6:13–20).

Since Jesus lives in our bodies and since He is God, we need to be sure He feels comfortable. We need to let Him call the shots, and we need to be sure we live according to His moral standards.

Reason #4: He Is Known Through My Body

Since God designed my body, purchased my body, and lives in my body, what I do with my body will reflect on Him. If I take good care of my body and modestly use each member of it according to God's loving limitations, I will represent an accurate picture of Jesus. But if I mess around morally and do things in my body which are off limits, I will communicate a distorted, twisted picture of Jesus. His reputation is at stake according to what I do in my body. When it becomes public knowledge that my body belongs to Jesus, He gets the credit for everything it accomplishes.

Betsy is one of the most popular girls in her sorority. I had always thought that she was an attractive girl, but one day I was with another guy who asked me, "What is it about Betsy that is so appealing?" I had never really thought about it before. Her hair is curly. Her eyes are big and droopy. Her nose is fat and her body is nothing to brag about. There is nothing physical that really makes her pretty.

After much discussion we decided that Betsy's spirit and her personality make her so beautiful. She is extremely happy and content with herself. She has accepted the person that God made her, and because she has accepted herself, others feel free to accept her as well. She has an inner beauty that is very attractive.

David, a student at Wheaton College, has cerebral palsy. David is one of the happiest, most radiant people on campus. He has had enough self-discipline to play four years of football and intends to go on to grad school. How can he do it when he has so many excuses just to lie back and feel sorry for himself? Because he loves himself and has accepted the person God has made. When you look at David, you don't feel sorry for him. He is actually an inspiration to the other students.

These two friends, David and Betsy, make me think of a verse in Proverbs, "A glad heart makes a cheerful countenance, but by sorrow of heart the spirit is broken" (*see* Proverbs 15:13).

Reason #5: He Wants to Control Our Bodies

Even though He could, God does not wrestle our lives out of our control. He is a Gentleman and He will not violate our dignity. Even though we rightfully belong to Him since He designed our bodies in the first place and then later purchased us to be His possessions, He will not manipulate us into submission. As we have seen, He loves us into submission. When we see Him bleeding, we want to obey Him but He leaves the choice up to us.

God knows that whatever controls our bodies controls our lives. A giant hunk of a man who yields his body to alcohol can be led around like a bull with a ring through his nose. A young woman who yields her body to cocaine can fall into such addiction that she is willing to do literally anything for a little bag of white powder.

This is why the Bible says, "Therefore do not let sin reign in your mortal body so that you obey its evil desires. Do not offer the parts of your body to sin, as instruments of wickedness, but rather offer yourselves to God, as those who have been brought from death to life; and offer the parts of your body to him as instruments of righteousness" (Romans 6:12, 13). "Therefore, I urge you, brothers, in view of God's mercy, to offer your bodies as living sacrifices, holy and pleasing to God—this is your spiritual act of worship" (Romans 12:1).

- God wants us to present our *eyes* to Him so that we use our eyes to look at things that are pure and creative and beautiful and profitable.
- He wants our *tongues* so that we speak words that are encouraging and inspirational, humorous and pleasant, which help others feel good about themselves.
- He wants control over our *ears* so that we listen to music that will set us in tune with Him.
- He wants our *minds* so that we think thoughts that are true and good and wholesome.
- He wants our *hands* so that we are involved in projects that are constructive and enduring.

- He wants our *feet* so that we hang around with people who will be a good influence on us and who will benefit by our relationship.
- He even wants our *sexuality* so that we will be examples of virginity, modesty, fidelity, and innocence.
- Most of all, He wants our *hearts* so that our deepest affections will flow to Him.

I'm Pretty Good

My body might not have the looks of Robert Redford, the coordination of Magic Johnson, and the brain of Albert Einstein but it is the body God wanted me to have.

My body might not have the eyebrows of Brooke Shields, the smile of Cheryl Tiegs, and the stamina of Jane Fonda, but whether I like it or not it is the body God custom made to fit me. It is one of a kind. We don't need to feel inferior as we look in the mirror because we don't need to compare ourselves with anyone else. As soon as I was made, He threw away the mold. Not only am I unique, but God has a unique message to give to others through me.

Regardless of what anyone else says about our bodies, we need to remind ourselves that we always have a secret admirer—God. He thinks we're pretty good.

For Discussion

1. When you meet a person of the opposite sex, what criteria do you use to judge him or her?

2. When other people meet you, by what are they impressed?
   What are your strengths?
   What makes a good impression?

3. When other people meet you, of what are they critical?
   What are your weaknesses?
   What makes a bad impression?

4. Have you ever had a nickname?
   Do people ever tease you for some physical flaw or lack of ability?

5. Why are our bodies important to God?
   What does it mean for God to be in control of my body?
   Why does He want to be in control of our bodies?
   How do we give God control of our bodies?
   • Of our hands?
   • Of our minds?
   • Of our feet?
   • Of our ears?
   • Of our eyes?
   • Of our tongues?

thirteen

I'm All Yours

Every one of us was born with a desire to love and trust another person with such intense passion that we could earnestly say with no strings attached, "I'm all yours." We each have a deep longing for intimacy that growls like a hunger pain. There is a restlessness that gnaws inside us until we find that special person who fulfills that desire.

I hate to pop the bubble but we will never find anyone who is capable of fulfilling this deep longing we feel inside. There is not a single person on the face of this planet who is complete enough to satisfy our cravings for intimacy. We also need to admit there is not a group of people who could somehow team up together and fulfill the silent screams of our hearts for that deeply personal relationship. "What a bummer!" you say. "What kind of sick God would create us with a desire that could never be fulfilled?"

There is one person who visited this planet upon whom we can completely cast ourselves and direct all our intense passions and affections toward without experiencing a nanosecond of disappointment—the Lord Jesus Christ. He wants every one of us to embrace Him heartily and shout with glee, "I'm all Yours!"

The Carving Knife

When my oldest son Fred was two years old, he waddled into the kitchen, reached his hand up on the counter, and before anyone noticed, he grabbed a carving knife around the blade. It was bright and shiny, and he thought he had found a real prize. He held it out toward his mother saying, "Look, mama!" My wife looked away and winced. She was scared.

I tried to take charge. "Listen to me, Fred, you give me that knife."

"No, no, dada," he said with a smile as his little fingers tightened around the blade. He put his arm behind his back as if he was hiding a fascinating treasure. To Fred it was a big game but to me it was highly dangerous.

I realized that if I tried to grab the knife from his grip, I would slice his tiny fingers and scar him for life. As his loving father I had to communicate to him that his bright shiny toy would be better in my hand. Someday when he got older I would teach him how to use it, but until then it would be better in my care. Eventually, he handed the knife to me and the game was over.

You and I have in our hands a very special treasure—our sexuality. Human sexuality is too big for us to keep in our custody. It is fascinating and certainly arouses our curiosity and it is something that we don't want to let go of. But we need to understand that sex is sacred. It is something far bigger than we are. As young adults we need to give it over to Jesus. We need to dedicate our bodies to Him—including our eyes, our hands, our ears, our tongues, our minds, our hearts, and our sex organs.

Just as my son handed over the bright, shiny carving knife to me as his loving father because he trusted me and realized I had his best interest in mind, so you and I can turn over our lives, bodies, and reputations to our loving heavenly Father. You and I can trust Him because He certainly has our best interests in mind.

Obviously turning over our lives, bodies, and reputations to Jesus is not quite as simple as handing over a carving knife. However, if we are willing, here is a model prayer which we can put in our own words:

> Jesus,
> I place my body on Your altar, and I want You to take complete control of it. I don't want to hold anything back from You.
> I give You my eyes and the things I look at.
> I give You my ears and the things I listen to.
> I give You my tongue and want You to help me speak only words that encourage and build up people.
> I give You my hands and my hobbies and interests.
> I give You my feet and all my friends. I don't ever want to be ashamed to let them know that my body belongs to You.

I give You my mind and desire to think only
things that are healthy

I give You my heart—every bit of it. I love You,
Jesus, above everything else, and I will always be
loyal to You regardless what everyone else is doing.

I give You my sexuality and my dating life. I will
submit to the loving limitations of Your moral law.
I am glad You have a strict standard to protect me.

Jesus, You died on the cross to purchase this body
of mine, so I want to live in such a way that when
people look at me they see You. Since You live inside
of me, please shine through me. I want You to get all
the credit for every good thing that comes from my
life. Praise You, Jesus

P.S. By the way, I just want You to know, I love
You and I think You are doing a great job being God.
I appreciate all You do, and I don't ever want to take
for granted all the fantastic things You are doing for
me. Thanks again.

Amen.

Hey, Take Good Care of My Reputation, Please

When we truly put Jesus first and everything else behind
Him, it's scary. *What if He blows it?* we wonder. *What if I put
my girlfriend in His control and she runs off and falls in love
with someone else?* We can't help but ask, *What if I hold to this
strict moral standard and my reputation goes down the tubes?*
These are all natural misgivings that we will feel when we
take Jesus seriously. In fact, I would suggest that if we do. 't
feel a little fearful as we turn our friends over to Jesus, we
probably don't understand what we are doing. He even said,
"Whoever acknowledges me before men, I will also acknowl-
edge him before my Father in heaven. But whoever disowns
me before men, I will disown him before my Father in heaven"
(Matthew 10: 32, 33). I always thought these words were a
little strong until I understood the logic. How can we think we
trust Jesus with our eternal salvation when we can't even trust
Him with our temporal reputation? Isn't that a little inconsis-
tent? When we truly believe Jesus can handle getting us to

heaven, we can certainly believe Him to get us through high school and college without a great deal of difficulty.

She Cried

When Sherry and I started dating we wanted to be sure our dating relationship was firmly rooted in healthy soil, so we started a Bible study just for the two of us. Two nights a week we met in the snack room in the basement of one of the campus dormitories, sat at a table with our Bibles open, and discussed what God was saying to us.

One night following a good study in Genesis 22 I was impressed by the love that Abraham had for God, which he clearly demonstrated when he willingly took his son, his only son, Isaac, whom he loved, and sacrificed him on an altar. Obviously Abraham did not kill his son, but he was willing to completely let him go to demonstrate that God came first.

Sherry and I wanted to prayerfully apply our study in a practical way. I paused and thought to myself, *What in my life right now is the most precious thing that I could give over to God?* All of a sudden a horrifying thought popped into my mind. *Give Sherry over to God.* Inside I gasped, *Oh, no, I can't do that!* God seemed to ask me, *Well then, how much do you love Me?*

I was caught. If I truly wanted to put God first, I needed to obey Him. I took Sherry by the hand, bowed my head, and sincerely prayed a prayer very similar to this one:

> Dear Jesus,
> Right now I give Sherry to You. I love You more than her. I don't ever want her to get in the way of my love for You and I never want to disrupt what You are doing in her life. If we are not right for each other, cause our love for each other to dry up. If I am not right for her, cause her to become more attracted to someone else. I give her completely to You and I put You first in my life.

I was afraid to say *amen*. I was even afraid to open my eyes to look at her as I thought she might be furious with me. After a few moments of silence I turned my head slightly and peeked out of one eye, looking across the table to her. To my amazement tears were running down her cheeks. Then she proceeded to pray a very similar prayer.

> Lord Jesus,
>   I give Fred to You. I never want to get in the way of Your best for him. If I am not the right person for him, make that clear to us or cause our love for each other to disappear. I know Fred is a special person, and I don't want to stand in the way of how You intend to use him. Jesus, I always want You to be number one in my life.

We did not know it at the time, but that little prayer did more to set our relationship down the right path than anything else we ever did together. Even though we did not pray together on a regular basis in order to avoid emotional intimacy, this notable exception stands out as a high point in our courtship.

I travel out of state once a month, sometimes for a week at a time. After returning home a few months ago I asked Sherry, "Do you ever get jealous of me? Do you ever wonder if I am being faithful to you when I'm in another city?" She said she doesn't. I told her I don't wonder about her either.

We discussed why it is that neither one of us has suffered from jealousy. We are both convinced that it traces back to the prayer we prayed in the basement of the college dormitory after our Bible study in Genesis 22. That prayer left an attitude in our hearts that has kept our relationship from getting greedy, ingrown, selfish, and possessive. When Jesus comes first, true unselfish love flows freely.

Love is openhanded. Love is kind and patient and self-giving. Love doesn't seek its own way. It doesn't look out for its own self-interests. Love believes all things, hopes all things, and endures all things (*see* 1 Corinthians 13). And greater love has no one than this: "To lay down one's life for a friend" (*see* John 15:13).

That night when Sherry and I turned over each other to

Jesus, we learned true love—love first for Jesus and then true love for each other. The faith we exercised that night has endured until now. We trust each other, but more than that we trust God with each other and that's special.

On the other hand, if we had held on to each other and refused to put Jesus first, we would be suspicious, jealous, and self-seeking. The tears Sherry shed that night have saved us both countless tears ever since.

True Friends

Having finished this book, perhaps you are saying to yourself, *You mean to tell me I have to dare to date differently?* The answer is emphatically NO! No one is trying to force you to date differently. There is no reason to be dragged kicking and screaming into the fascinating world of dating. My advice is, please keep an open mind and don't pretend to have all the answers. Someday you might be looking for an alternative at which time this book might be worth dusting off.

Or perhaps, having finished this book some of you are saying to yourselves, *Wow, you mean to tell me I can dare to date differently?* The answer is emphatically YES! For those who have been looking for an alternative, I hope you are glad to find one and are now prepared to rise to the occasion.

It is difficult to say when it happens or what causes it to happen but it is a wonderful change when we move from saying, "You mean I *have* to?" to saying, "You mean I *get* to?" It is only a change in attitude and yet turning that corner puts us on an entirely new street.

When we move from asking, "What can I *get away with* and still be a Christian?" and start asking, "What can I *give up* to be a better Christian?" we are entering into the big leagues. We are not far from becoming pacesetters and moral leaders. When we move from being embarrassed that our bodies belong to Jesus to being grateful and excited that our bodies belong to Him, we are eligible to be among the moral revolutionaries who will bring answers to our confused generation.

Rather than fighting against God's moral law as an obstacle

to our fun, when we take delight in His moral law as the means to our freedom, we move into a deeply intimate and personal friendship with Jesus and He calls us friends. "You are my friends if you do what I command. I no longer call you servants, because a servant does not know his master's business. Instead, I have called you friends, for everything that I learned from my Father I have made known to you" (John 15: 14, 15).

With Jesus as our number-one Friend, we can have the courage to climb out of the dating rut and start dancing to the beat of a different drum. We don't need to simply copy the outdated methods of courtship that we observe around us We can *dare to date differently*.

For Discussion

1. Finish the sentence, "A friend is. . . ."
   See how long a list of characteristics you can make.

2. Why is it frightening to turn over our reputations to God?
   What are we afraid of?
   Why are our reputations so important to us?

3. Before the author was married, he held Sherry's hand, bowed his head, prayed, and gave her to God. When he opened his eyes, to his surprise she was crying.
   Why did she cry?
   Why was he surprised?
   What does this story tell us about true love?

4. Why is it important for us to turn our reputations over to God?

5. What is the difference between asking God, "You mean I *have* to?" and asking Him, "You mean I *get* to?"

6. In what ways can Jesus be your Friend?

Ten Good Questions and Honest Answers

QUESTION #1: *"What should I say when my boyfriend tells me that if I loved him, I'd go to bed with him?"*

The next time someone says, "If you loved me, you'd go to bed with me," respond by saying, "If you loved me, you wouldn't ask such a thing."

The Bible says, "Love is patient and kind" (*see* 1 Corinthians 13:4). True love is willing to wait until marriage, because it recognizes that love means more than a twenty-minute sizzle in the backseat of a car. True love respects the worth and dignity of the other person too much to defraud his or her moral integrity.

QUESTION #2: *"Isn't it okay to have sex, since we're planning to get married soon anyway? We're committed to each other, since we love each other. What difference does a piece of paper make?"*

It might sound harsh, but if you are not married, you are not committed. That is what marriage is—commitment. Marriage is the publicly witnessed legal commitment binding a man and a woman. Anything less is not a marriage commitment.

The Bible says, ". . . She is your companion and your wife by covenant" (Malachi 2:14 RSV). How did she become your wife? By covenant. If a man and a woman are ready to make a commitment to each other, they should get married. Prior to that public vow, there is not the commitment necessary to provide the healthy protection needed to preserve sexual activity.

QUESTION #3: *"Is God just trying to ruin a good time?"*

We have all had the desire to get close to someone we really like. The idea that God has placed limitations on our sexual activity might sound as though He is trying to keep us from pleasure, but actually He is trying to keep us from pain. To say that sex outside marriage is fun is only half the truth. The Bible admits there are fleeting pleasures of sin (Hebrews 11:25), but it also warns that the wages of sin are death and pain (Romans 6:23). God gives loving, logical limitations to sexual activity, because He wants to save us from all the headaches and heartaches of overextended relationships.

QUESTION #4: *"Don't Christians just have a low view of sex?"*

Christians do not believe that *sex* is a dirty word. We believe it is a holy word. This is precisely why we do not take off our clothes in public or look at pictures of others who have taken off their clothes. This is why we do not tell sex jokes or laugh when others tell them. This is why we do not sleep around with Joe Blow or Sally Sweetlips.

Every society establishes laws to protect that which it values. If we value private property, we will establish laws to prosecute thieves. If we value human life, we will prosecute murderers. Since we value human sexuality, we maintain standards that reserve sex for the marriage bed exclusively.

QUESTION #5: *"We've known each other for so long, won't our relationship die if it doesn't develop sexually?"*

In reality, nothing kills a good relationship faster than messing around with each other's bodies. Once couples become sexually involved prior to marriage, the relationship has begun to self-destruct.

I live in south Florida, where we grow coconut palms. I have learned an interesting fact about coconuts. Inside the hard outer shell is very tender white meat and very sweet coconut milk. However, if the coconut is not ripe, the milk can be poisonous. If you pick the coconuts too soon, the milk could be lethal. Thousands of teenagers have become sexually active too soon and ruined their relationships because of it. The Bible says, "Passion rots the bones" (*see* Proverbs 14:30) and can destroy a perfectly good relationship.

If you have known each other for a long time, you need to follow some commonsense guidelines.

- *Stay recreationally active:* tennis, basketball, jogging.
- *Stay socially active:* maintain other friendships and group activities.
- *Avoid overexposure:* Don't spend too much time together and avoid being alone for an extended time.
- *Do service projects together for other people:* Mow the lawn for an elderly person, take a lonely kid to the park.

QUESTION #6:   *"Can't I be sexually active and still go to heaven?"*

To be candid, most people who ask this are either fakers or failures. A faker is a non-Christian who acts like a Christian. When fakers die they go to hell.

God doesn't want us to see how close we can walk to the edge without falling over. He wants us to stay away from the edge altogether. We need to understand that if we live like hell, chances are we will go there. (We can read it for ourselves: Galatians 5:19–21; 6:7, 8; 1 Thessalonians 4:3–8; 1 Corinthians 6:9, 10; Ephesians 5:5.)

A failure is a Christian who at times acts like a non-Christian. A Christian might be currently involved in an immoral relationship, but God loves him too much to leave him there. God's love is not only able to forgive him for past sin, but deliver him from present and future sin. When a failure dies he goes to heaven.

Again, "Can't I be sexually active and still go to heaven?" Yes, it is possible. However, it is also quite possible that you will not go to heaven. In either case, God does not want us to be sexually active outside of marriage. He doesn't even want us to desire being sexually active outside of marriage.

QUESTION #7:   *"Is there any reason why I should date only Christians?"*

Suggesting that we use guidelines in selecting who we should and should not date is like touching a sacred cow. People get offended and emotionally fired up.

Michelle was a popular student. She was easy to talk with and always had something nice to say. She was a solid Christian, committed to living for Jesus. When she came back to school after spring break, her senior year, and told her friends she was engaged to a non-Christian, they didn't know whether to laugh or cry. They tried to talk with her about it, but it was too late.

"Hey, we love each other," she insisted. "It will work out. My parents were married before my dad was a Christian, and it worked out for them. Besides, he's too good a catch to let him go. After all, I am a senior, and I don't want to graduate as an old maid."

Sometime after the wedding Michelle realized everything was not as smooth as she thought. Her new husband's life was based on a value system categorically different from her own. On Sundays all he wanted to do was golf, play tennis, or go to the beach. Their refrigerator was always stocked with beer, and it didn't take her long to realize that his idea of a wife was someone to fix meals, have sex with, and otherwise stay out of his way. Every day they would argue, and every day she would cry. She was afraid to talk with her old friends, because they had told her not to marry him in the first place. She couldn't share her feelings with her parents, because she felt as if she had to keep up a good front. By the time she came to me for help, their marriage was already badly damaged. Michelle knew she had made a big mistake, and she felt trapped.

I share Michelle's story because she asked me to. The last time we met together she said, "Hey, Fred, if there is any way my situation can keep others from making the same mistake I did, please share it."

Too many of us still think we can break the rules and not get caught. God has set down definite limitations on who we should and should not date. He has lovingly done this, not to keep us from pleasure, but in order to keep us from pain. Michelle got intimate with a guy who had a completely different value system, and it kept her from thinking straight until it was too late. It would not have happened if she refused to date non-Christians.

It is best to date only Christians. God forbids marrying non-Christians (Deuteronomy 7:3; Ezra 10; Malachi 2:11; 2 Corinthians 6:14–17). Obviously, not everyone who dates a non-Christian will eventually marry that person, but Michelle learned the hard way that it can happen.

"Yeah," many girls object, "but I've dated non-Christian guys who treated me better than Christian guys."

I agree. Worse than dating a moral non-Christian is dating an immoral Christian. Guys who parade like spiritual giants while at church, yet act like moral slobs while on dates turn God off. The two words *immoral* and *Christian* should never be used together.

The Apostle Paul gave his younger friend Timothy some sound dating advice, "Flee youthful lusts and aim at righteousness, faith, love and peace along with those who call upon the Lord from a pure heart" (*see* 2 Timothy 2:22). He actually gives two guidelines in selecting possible dates: Only *Christians* ("those who call upon the name of the Lord") who are *morally pure* ("pure heart"). Even if a non-Christian acts morally, his moral standard is not based on the authority of the Bible, so his convictions could crumble when temptations increase. Therefore, God suggests for us not to date non-Christians. In addition, even Christians who do not hold to strict moral standards are to be considered off limits and potentially hazardous.

QUESTION #8: *"Is there anything wrong with having non-Christian friends?"*

Absolutely not. Jesus was called "a friend of sinners." If it was wrong to have non-Christian friends, then He sure blew it. We need to show the love of Jesus to those who do not yet know Him.

The Bible does say, however, "Bad company corrupts good character" (1 Corinthians 15:33). Since dating relationships are potentially intimate, they make us vulnerable. The possibility of bad company corrupting good character is never greater than in a dating situation. For this reason we are told to date only Christians who have strict moral standards. However, this does not mean that we should stick our heads in the sand and cut ourselves off from all our non-Christian friends.

It helps us to realize there are several levels of friends: Acquaintances, whom we know by name; casual friends, with whom we share hobbies, interests, and limited activities; close friends with whom we share personal feelings and extensive activities; and intimate friends, with whom we share values and life goals. We still probably only have a half-dozen intimate friends in a lifetime. If we are Christians, it is obvious that our intimate friends can only be fellow Christians, because they are the only friends with whom we share common values and life goals. There is, however, no reason to avoid casual friendships with non-Christians.

Every year I receive a fistful of letters from parents complaining about how their teenagers' friends negatively influence them. Some parents move from one neighborhood to another, just to change school districts, so their son or daughter might be uprooted from "bad friends."

I tell parents that the problem is probably not with their teenagers' friends. The problem is probably with their teenager. We enjoy a certain group of friends because we vibrate together. "Birds of a feather flock together." As young people it is time to quit blaming others for our activities and to start assuming responsibility for ourselves. If we enjoy smoking marijuana, drinking alcohol, or messing around morally in one school district, we will find friends with similar interests in the new school district. The problem is not with the school district, the problem is with us. We don't need a change of friends; we need a change of heart.

QUESTION #9: *"Is masturbation a sin?"*

(Maybe I should answer a more basic question first: "What is masturbation?" It is a person's rubbing of his or her genitals [sex organs] until he or she experiences a tingling sensation.)

Two different answers have traditionally been given to the question "Is masturbation a sin?" and both miss the point. Some used horrible scare tactics in an attempt to stamp out masturbation. They said it caused blindness, mental illness, baldness, and infertility. How ridiculous! Masturbation is not the unforgivable sin, and it does not have any such physical side effects. Others claim masturbation is a normal part of growing up and is morally neutral—neither good nor bad. While this view is closer to the truth, it does not consider all the facts.

Masturbation is common. Presumably 95 percent of all teenagers masturbate during adolescence. However, most teenagers also lie sometime during adolescence, and while lying is certainly not the unforgivable sin, neither is it acceptable behavior. Since God's standard is based on *no lust,* and planned appeals to lustful desires are off limits, masturbating, which includes planned sexual arousal, is also off limits.

As a Christian young person, you will probably face temptation to masturbate. If you give in, Jesus still loves you; He will forgive you, and you will not suffer any physical damage. There is, however, a more exciting option than giving in to the temptation and getting hooked on a bad habit. I know dozens of young men and women across the country who have experienced wonderful victory over this problem. Jesus can set us free from masturbation. Here are some helpful guidelines:

- Tell Jesus you have the problem and that you want to stop.
- Agree with Him that deliberately arousing lustful desire is wrong.
- Thank Him for dying on the cross, being raised from the dead, and living in you. Thank Him for loving you just the way you are, and thank Him for giving you power to obey Him.
- Memorize some fitting verses to use as power boosters in resisting the temptation whenever you have evil thoughts. (*See* Appendix II.)
- Tell Jesus that your body belongs to Him, and ask Him to keep the enemy (Satan) from you.
- Ask God for a constructive, healthy project into which you can immediately invest your energies (write a letter to a friend, read the Bible, go talk to your parents, telephone someone you haven't seen for a while, jog around the block). First Peter 4:2 suggests that we don't need to live the rest of our lives ". . . for evil desires, but rather for the will of God." When tempted physically, get up, leave the room you are in, and do something else.
- Thank God that He has given you victory over this temptation. Rather than wasting your energies on ingrown self-stimulation, He has helped you channel yourself in constructive service.

QUESTION #10:   *"But how can I feel forgiven?"*

When I don't feel forgiven, I face a simple decision, *Who will I believe: my feelings or God's Word?*

The Bible plainly says, "If we confess our sins, he is faithful and just and will forgive us our sins . . ." (1 John 1:9). That is a promise. It is based on God's faithfulness, not our feelings.

Again, the Bible says, "Do not call anything impure that God has made clean" (Acts 10:15). If God calls me clean, I should not keep calling myself impure. I need to trust Him and believe what He says.

Appendix II

Power Boosters

These Bible verses are exciting to memorize. They are power boosters to be quoted whenever we face pressure to compr mise our convictions, when we are all alone, on a date, or in a group.

"Do not let this Book of the Law depart from your mouth; meditate on it day and night, so that you may be careful to do everything written in it. Then you will be prosperous and successful. Have I not commanded you? Be strong and courageous. Do not be terrified; do not be discouraged, for the Lord your God will be with you wherever you go."
Joshua 1:8, 9

"I made a covenant with my eyes not to look lustfully at a girl."

Job 31:1

Blessed is the man who does not walk in the counsel of the wicked or stand in the way of sinners or sit in the seat of mockers. But his delight is in the law of the Lord, and on his law he meditates day and night. He is like a tree planted by streams of water, which yields its fruit in season and whose leaf does not wither. Whatever he does prospers.

Psalms 1:1–3

... I will walk in my house with blameless heart. I will set before my eyes no vile thing. ...
Psalms 101:2, 3

How can a young man keep his way pure? By living according to your word. I seek you with all my heart; do not let me stray from your commands. I have hidden your word in my heart that I might not sin against you.
Psalms 119:9–11

Can a man scoop fire into his lap without his clothes being burned? Can a man walk on hot coals without his feet being scorched?

Proverbs 6:27, 28

A tranquil mind gives life to the flesh, but passion makes the bones rot.

Proverbs 14:30 RSV

"You have heard that it was said, 'Do not commit adultery.' But I tell you that anyone who looks at a woman lustfully has already committed adultery with her in his heart. If your right eye causes you sin, gouge it out and throw it away. It is better for you to lose one part of your body than for your whole body to be thrown into hell."

Matthew 5:27–29

"Enter through the narrow gate. For wide is the gate and broad is the road that leads to destruction, and many enter through it. But small is the gate and narrow the road that leads to life, and only a few find it."

Matthew 7:13, 14

Do not offer the parts of your body to sin, as instruments of wickedness, but rather offer yourselves to God, as those who have been brought from death to life; and offer the parts of your body to him as instruments of righteousness. For sin shall not be your master, because you are not under law, but under grace.

Romans 6:13, 14

Do you not know that the wicked will not inherit the kingdom of God? Do not be deceived: Neither the sexually immoral nor idolators nor adulterers nor male prostitutes nor homosexual offenders nor thieves nor the greedy nor drunkards nor slanderers nor swindlers will inherit the kingdom of God.

1 Corinthians 6:9, 10

Flee from sexual immorality. All other sins a man commits are outside his body, but he who sins sexually sins against his own body. Do you not know that your body is a temple of the Holy Spirit, who is in you, whom you have received from God? You are not your own; you were bought at a price. Therefore honor God with your body.

1 Corinthians 6:18–20

No temptation has seized you except what is common to man. And God is faithful; he will not let you be tempted beyond what you can bear. But when you are tempted, he will also provide a way out so that you can stand up under it.

1 Corinthians 10:13

"Therefore come out from them and be separate, says the Lord. Touch no unclean thing, and I will receive you. I will be a Father to you, and you will be my sons and daughters, says the Lord Almighty." Since we have these promises, dear friends, let us purify ourselves from everything that contaminates body and spirit, perfecting holiness out of reverence for God.

2 Corinthians 6:17–7:1

So I say, live by the Spirit, and you will not gratify the desires of the sinful nature. For the sinful nature desires what is contrary to the Spirit, and the Spirit what is contrary to the sinful nature. They are in conflict with each other, so that you do not do what you want. But if you are led by the Spirit, you are not under law. The acts of the sinful nature are obvious: sexual immorality, impurity and debauchery; idolatry and witchcraft; hatred, discord, jealousy, fits of rage, selfish ambition, dissensions, factions and envy; drunkenness, orgies, and the like. I warn you, as I did before, that those who live like this will not inherit the kingdom of God.

Galatians 5:16–21

Do not be deceived: God cannot be mocked. A man reaps what he sows. The one who sows to please his sinful nature, from that nature will reap destruction; the one who sows to please the Spirit, from the Spirit will reap eternal life.

Galatians 6:7, 8

But among you there must not be even a hint of sexual immorality, or of any kind of impurity, or of greed, because these are improper for God's holy people. Nor should there be obscenity, foolish talk or coarse joking, which are out of place, but rather thanksgiving. For of this you can be sure: No immoral, impure or greedy person—such a man is an idolater—has any inheritance in the kingdom of Christ and of God.

Ephesians 5:3–5

Put to death, therefore, whatever belongs to your earthly nature: sexual immorality, impurity, lust, evil desires and greed, which is idolatry. Because of these, the wrath of God is coming. You used to walk in these ways, in the life you once lived. But now you must rid yourselves of all such things as these: anger, rage, malice, slander, and filthy language from your lips.

Colossians 3:5–8

Let the word of Christ dwell in you richly as you teach and admonish one another with all wisdom, and as you sing psalms, hymns and spiritual songs with gratitude in your hearts to God.

Colossians 3:16

And whatever you do, whether in word or deed, do it all in the name of the Lord Jesus, giving thanks to God the Father through him.

Colossians 3:17

It is God's will that you should be sanctified: that you should avoid sexual immorality; that each of you should learn to control his own body in a way that is holy and honorable, not in passionate lust like the heathen, who do not know God; and that in this matter no one should wrong his brother or take advantage of him. The Lord will punish men for all such sins, as we have already told you and warned you. For God did not call us to be impure, but to live a holy life. Therefore, he who rejects this instruction does not reject man but God, who gives you his Holy Spirit.

1 Thessalonians 4:3–8

For God did not give us a spirit of timidity, but a spirit of power, of love and of self-discipline.

2 Timothy 1:7

Flee the evil desires of youth, and pursue righteousness, faith, love and peace, along with those who call on the Lord out of a pure heart.

2 Timothy 2:22

Marriage should be honored by all, and the marriage bed kept pure, for God will judge the adulterer and all the sexually immoral

Hebrews 13:4

Submit yourselves, then, to God. Resist the devil, and he will flee from you. Come near to God and he will come near to you. Wash your hands, you sinners, and purify your hearts, you double-minded.

James 4:7, 8

Be self-controlled and alert. Your enemy the devil prowls around like a roaring lion looking for someone to devour. Resist him, standing firm in the faith, because you know that your brothers throughout the world are undergoing the same kind of sufferings. And the God of all grace, who called you to his eternal glory in Christ, after you have suffered a little while, will himself restore you and make you strong, firm and steadfast.

1 Peter 5:8–10

For this very reason, make every effort to add to your faith goodness; and to goodness, knowledge; and to knowledge, self-control; and to self-control, perseverance; and to perseverance, godliness; and to godliness, brotherly kindness; and to brotherly kindness, love. For if you possess these qualities in increasing measure, they will keep you from being ineffective and unproductive in your knowledge of our Lord Jesus Christ. But if anyone does not have them, he is nearsighted and blind, and has forgotten that he has been cleansed from his past sins. Therefore, my brothers, be all the more eager to make your calling and

election sure. For if you do these things, you will never
fall.

2 Peter 1:5–10

I write to you, fathers, because you have known him who
is from the beginning. I write to you, young men, because
you are strong, and the word of God lives in you, and you
have overcome the evil one.

1 John 2:14

To him who is able to keep you from falling and to present
you before his glorious presence without fault and with
great joy—to the only God our Savior be glory, majesty,
power and authority. . . .

Jude 24, 25

Then I heard another voice from heaven say: "Come out of
her, my people, so that you will not share in her sins, so
that you will not receive any of her plagues; for her sins
are piled up to heaven, and God has remembered her
crimes."

Revelation 18:4, 5

"Blessed are those who wash their robes, that they may
have the right to the tree of life and may go through the
gates into the city. Outside are the dogs, those who
practice magic arts, the sexually immoral, the murderers,
the idolators and everyone who loves and practices falsehood."

Revelation 22:14

Premarital Analysis

Name _____

Age _____

1. I am living: (a) at home, (b) at school, (c) with a friend, (d) in my own apartment.

2. My family's response to my fiancé(e): (a) strong dislike, (b) tolerance, (c) approval, (d) strong favoring.

3. My parents: (a) wish we would wait to marry, (b) have expressed hesitations, (c) don't have feelings either way, (d) approve our marriage at this time.

4. My view of premarital sex: (a) it's fine as long as you love each other, (b) it's find as long as you don't get carried away, (c) makes me feel guilty; I know I shouldn't, (d) I know it is wrong and that God has given me strength to wait until marriage.

5. My view of divorce: (a) it depends on the circumstances, (b) I hope it doesn't happen to me, (c) God hates divorce, and I know marriage is a permanent commitment.

6. Define *love*.

7. What makes your love for your fiancé(e) different from your love for anyone else?

8. What is marriage?

9. What fears and apprehensions do you have toward marriage?

10. Why do you feel *now* is the best time to get married?

11. From God's point of view (according to the Bible), is there a difference between the role of a husband and the role of the wife? (Yes/no—circle one.) If so, what are the differences?

12. How will these role distinctions make a difference in your marriage?

13. Roles/responsibilities (His—1, hers—5, ours—3)
    • Provide financially
    • Balance a checkbook
    • Do grocery shopping
    • Wash the car
    • Mow the lawn
    • Buy a new car
    • Do the dishes
    • Change diapers
    • Cook dinner
    • Discipline children
    • Read Scriptures

14. What sexual experiences have you had? Is this known by your fiancé(e)? Are you sexually active with your fiancé(e)?

15. How many children do you want? Does your partner agree?

16. Are you more a talker or a listener? Are you moody? Is your fiancé(e) moody?

17. Is your fiancé(e) too close to either parent?

18. Who are you closer to, your mother or your father? How do you feel toward that parent?

19. In what ways do you plan to change your mate?

20. Have you planned a budget? Will you have one checking account or two?

21. What do you like most about your fiancé(e)? What do you like least? (What bugs you?)

22. Who is more spiritual?

23. Who is more intellectual?

Appendix IV

The Total-Person Filter

We are complex individuals. It is good for us to become whole people—strong and vibrant in many areas of life. We can determine how healthy a dating relationship is according to how we are developing in each area.

1. While dating these areas will develop and mature in a healthy relationship.

- *Socially:* Do I still see my old friends, or do I spend all my time with my girlfriend (boyfriend)?
  Do we do things together with other friends, or are we off by ourselves?
- *Personally (family):* Do I spend time with my parents, or am I always with my girlfriend (boyfriend)?
  Do I tell more secrets to my parents or to my girlfriend (boyfriend)?
- *Mentally:* Do we talk a lot and challenge each other mentally, or do we just sit and make out?
  Do we discuss issues, or do we dominate what the other person thinks?
- *Recreationally:* Are we active in sports (bike riding, skiing, tennis, jogging, roller-skating) or do we just watch TV or play video games?
- *Spiritually:* Do we read the Bible more or less than when we first started dating?
  Do I enjoy attending church more or less than when we first started dating?

2. While engaged this area will develop the most.

- *Emotionally:* Obviously our emotions will be involved during dating, but they must be kept under control. During engagement, however, we can pop the cork and let the juices flow more freely. We have already asked for and received parental permission for marriage. We have set a marriage date. The intention of commitment has been expressed. Now we can enjoy much praying together and great joy in the purity of premarriage courtship.

3. The *wedding night* is when the final area is experienced.

• *Physically:* Having waited until marriage, we can now enjoy the physical exchange of love. The Bible says, "Drink water from your own cistern, running water from your own well. Should your springs overflow in the streets, your streams of water in the public squares? Let them be yours alone, never to be shared with strangers. May your fountain be blessed, and may you rejoice in the wife of your youth. A loving doe, a graceful deer—may her breasts satisfy you always, may you ever be captivated by her love" (Proverbs 5:15–19).

Sexual intercourse is a wonderful expression of love between husband and wife. It is sacred, holy. It is joyous, exciting, exhilarating. It is beyond description. It is well worth the wait.

We can try to break the rules and reverse the sequence, but we will not enjoy the fullness of life God intended. Dating was intended to be done God's way. If we disregard His guidelines we will miss the excitement. However, if we date according to the rules and sincerely desire to please Him, our strict moral standards will be doorways to help us to happiness rather than fences which hinder it.

Appendix V

How to Break Up

While writing this book I have felt much like a big brother talking with my younger brothers and sisters about some very personal, intimate concerns. Before we finish I feel like putting my arm around your shoulder, looking you in the eyes, and asking you if there is anything you would like to tell me about where you are at with this whole area of sex and morals and dating.

Perhaps you are currently involved in a raunchy relationship. Initially it might have been promising, but you became sexually involved, and things have gone downhill. You now realize the relationship is rotting on the vine, and you want out.

Jesus taught, "You have heard that it was said, 'Do not commit adultery.' But I tell you that anyone who looks at a woman lustfully has already committed adultery with her in his heart. If your right eye causes you to sin, gouge it out and throw it away. It is better for you to lose one part of your body than for your whole body to be thrown into hell. And if your right hand causes you to sin, cut it off and throw it away. It is better for you to lose one part of your body than for your whole body to go into hell" (Matthew 5:27–30).

Unfortunately, many have misunderstood what Jesus meant by plucking out eyes and cutting off hands. In Baton Rouge, Louisiana, a twenty-six-year-old woman is being charged with pulling a boy's eye out of its socket and leaving it hanging on the cheek by nothing more than the optic nerve. Allegedly she was praying over the boy, who lusted after women and looked at pornography, as she quoted these verses from the Bible.

I hope we all understand Jesus is not advocating maiming ourselves or anyone else. Primarily He is telling us that our moral condition is more important than our eyesight or our mobility. As much as we value the use of our eyes and hands, we should put greater value on our moral purity and fidelity.

Jesus is also teaching us that in order for us to avoid lustful, raunchy relationships we, at times, will need to perform radical surgery. I know a young woman who lived with a man outside of marriage for years. When she turned her life over to Jesus, she knew the relationship needed to end. It required radical surgery. As painful as it was to cut it off, she chose to follow Jesus down the righteous highway.

I want you to do something gross: *Think back to the last time you vomited.* Can you remember what you ate prior to getting sick to your stomach? Can you remember what chunks of partially digested food were looking up at you?

Often the food you ate prior to vomiting is repulsive to you for months afterwards. If you ate spaghetti and saw a pile of partially digested noodles lying on the floor, you will not feel like eating spaghetti for a while. If you ate Chinese food and saw bean sprouts and rice lying in the sink, you would not have much of an appetite for chow mein next time.

There come times when raunchy relationships become so nauseating that we want to do nothing more than vomit them up. We are so sick of them, we never want to taste the stuff again.

The problem is not with the persons we are dating. They are not like bad food. The problem is with us. Sin has destroyed the relationship, and it is too late to salvage it. It is time to blow the whistle and say the game is over. Here is how.

- *Start with God.* Tell Him what went wrong and agree with Him that it needs to stop.
- *Get alone.* Think through how you sinned against the person you were dating. Figure out which primary sins prompted the moral problem: (a) pride, (b) insensitivity, (c) lack of love.
- *Write it down.* Decide on the right wording as you need to ask for forgiveness. "As we have been dating I know I have been wrong. Will you forgive me for the sin of. . . ." Ask forgiveness in a manner that will not point the finger at the other person's sin. Keep asking until he or she says, "Yes, I forgive you."
- *Telephone.* After that person forgives you, say, "My body belongs to Jesus, and I know I can't handle the

relationship anymore. I sincerely want God's best for you, but we can't see each other any longer. It hurts me, and I care for you very much, but we cannot date each other any more."

• *Flashbacks.* I guarantee you, at least one hundred times you will want to call, visit, write a note, and date this special person, after you break up. He or she might persist in reaching out to you. If you are a young woman, you might have that guy cry and appeal to your motherly instincts. He might tell you he needs you, deserves you, will die without you. Such appeals are weak, manipulative, and off limits. Though you will feel guilty of harsh treatment when you refuse these appeals, you are not guilty. In such cases love must be tough. It is far more loving to submit to God's loving limitations than to give in to the pressure of a boyfriend. If you truly love a person, you will do what is right even if at the time he does not understand.

It is not righteous for a woman to express her motherly instincts prior to being a mother. Nor is it righteous for a man to express his fatherly, protective instincts prior to being a father. At times young men will feel justified in extending a dead relationship for the sake of saving a girl from an abusive homelife or some other tragedy. Such a sacrifice sounds noble, but is usually better expressed by making arrangements for someone else to help. When a relationship needs to end, excuses are easy to find, but what we need is the honesty to simply say, "Hey, I care very much for you, and that is why we can't date anymore."